CATHOLICISM
& ORTHODOX CHRISTIANITY
WORLD RELIGIONS

by
Stephen F. Brown and Khaled Anatolios

☑® Facts On File, Inc.

CATHOLICISM & Orthodox Christianity
World Religions

Facts On File, Inc.
132 West 31st Street
New York NY 10001

Library of Congress Cataloging-in-Publication Data
Brown, Stephen F.
    Catholicism & Orthodox Christianity / by Stephen F. Brown and
    Khaled Anatolios
        p. cm. — (World religions)
    Includes bibliographical references (p. 125) and index.
    ISBN 0-8160-4613-1
    1. Orthodox Eastern Church—Relations—Catholic Church—History. 2. Catholic Church—Relations—Orthodox Eastern Church—History. I. Anatolios, Khaled 1962. II. Title. III. Series.
    BX324.3 .B76 2001   2001040277
    280'.2'09–dc21

Facts On File books are available at special discounts when purchased in bulk quantities for businesses, associations, institutions or sales promotions. Please call our Special Sales Department in New York at (212) 967-8800 or (800) 322-8755.

You can find Facts On File on the World Wide Web at http://www.factsonfile.com

Developed by Brown Publishing Network, Inc. Series design by Trelawney Goodell. Design Production by Jennifer J. Angell/ Brown Publishing Network, Inc. Photo Research by Susan Van Etten.

Photo credits:

Cover: Stained Glass Window of unknown origin, Italy ©Larry Chiger/Superstock; *Title page*: Adoration of the Kings, Matteo di Giovanni/©Bettmann/CORBIS; *Table of Contents page*: Crucifixion, Sassoferrato/©Arte & Immagini srl/CORBIS; *Pages 6–7*: ©David Lees/CORBIS; *9*: ©Richard T. Nowitz/CORBIS; *12*: ©Adam Woolfit/CORBIS; *16*: ©Michael S. Yamashita/CORBIS; *22–23*: Adoration of the Shepherds, Murillo/©Gianni Dagli/CORBIS; *30*: ©Edimedia/CORBIS; *32*: ©Bettmann/CORBIS; *34–35*: ©David Lees/CORBIS; *37*: ©Philadelphia Museum of Art/CORBIS; *40*: ©Bettmann/CORBIS; *42*: ©Bettmann/CORBIS; *45*: ©Bettmann/CORBIS; *51*: ©Archivo Iconografico, S.A./COR-BIS; *56*: ©Morton Beebe/CORBIS; *61*: Courtesy, Greek Orthodox Diocese of Boston; *62*: ©AFP/CORBIS; *64–65*: ©AFP/CORBIS; *68*: ©Jose F. Poblete/CORBIS; *75*: ©*GOD WITH US PUBLICATIONS (Kindergarten Book)*, Pittsburgh, PA; *76*: ©Catholic News Service; *79*: ©Owen Franken/CORBIS; *80*: ©Michael S. Yamashita/CORBIS; *83*: ©Reuters NewMedia Inc/CORBIS; *84*: ©Dave Bartruff/CORBIS; *86–87*: ©Bettmann/CORBIS; *89*: ©Jonathan Blair/CORBIS; *91*: ©Alinari/Art Resource, NY; *92*: ©Michael Brennan/CORBIS; *95*: ©Kee Publishing Services, Ltd/CORBIS; *96*: ©Susan Van Etten; *99*: ©Art & Immagini srl/CORBIS; *104*: ©AFP/CORBIS; *108–109*: ©Reuters NewMedia Inc/CORBIS; *112*: ©AFP/CORBIS; *115*: ©Owen Franken/CORBIS; *118*: Hulton-Deutsch Collection/COR-BIS; *120*: ©Jeffrey Rotman/CORBIS.

Printed in the United States of America

VB 10 9 8 7 6 5 4 3

This book is printed on acid-free paper.

TABLE OF CONTENTS

Preface

The 20th century is sometimes called a "secular age," meaning, in effect, that religion is not an especially important issue for most people. But there is much evidence to suggest that this is not true. In many societies, including the United States, religion and religious values shape the lives of millions of individuals and play a key role in politics and culture as well.

The World Religions series, of which this book is a part, is designed to appeal to both students and general readers. The books offer clear, accessible overviews of the major religious traditions and institutions of our time. Each volume in the series describes where a particular religion is practiced, its origins and history, its central beliefs and important rituals, and its contributions to world civilization. Carefully chosen photographs complement the text, and a glossary and bibliography are included to help readers gain a more complete understanding of the subject at hand.

Religious institutions and spirituality have always played a central role in world history. These books will help clarify what religion is all about and reveal both the similarities and differences in the great spiritual traditions practiced around the world today.

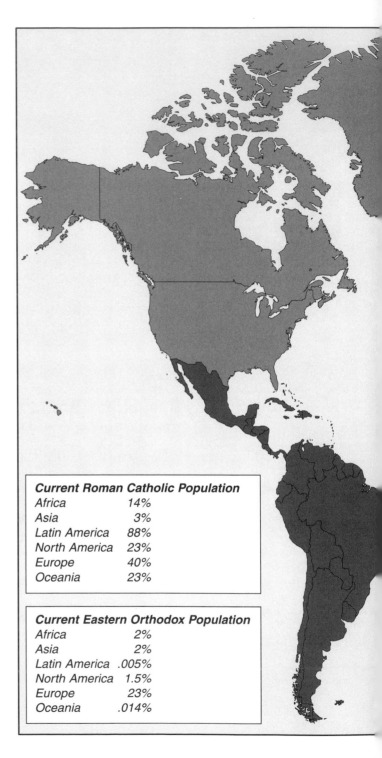

Current Roman Catholic Population

Africa	14%
Asia	3%
Latin America	88%
North America	23%
Europe	40%
Oceania	23%

Current Eastern Orthodox Population

Africa	2%
Asia	2%
Latin America	.005%
North America	1.5%
Europe	23%
Oceania	.014%

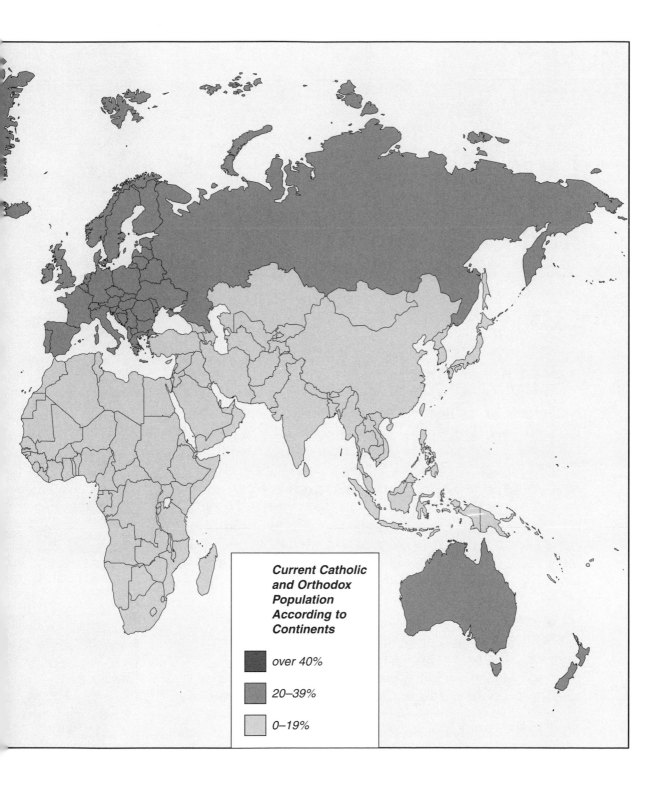

Current Catholic and Orthodox Population According to Continents

over 40%

20–39%

0–19%

CHAPTER 1

Introduction:
The Modern Catholic
and Orthodox Worlds

When people think of the Catholic Church, they generally think of the Roman Catholic Church. They may imagine the pope leading a group of youngsters in song at a Paris stadium, or pleading for a Millennium Year rededication to Christian values in Rome, or kissing a basket of Greek soil and olive branches at the airport upon his arrival in Athens.

Closer to home, people may see in newspapers the picture of a bishop celebrating a religious feast in a local cathedral, or even know Catholics in their neighborhood attending Saint John's School or working at Saint Elizabeth's Hospital. They may be aware of a soup kitchen run in a church or an AIDS hospice located in a building next to the cathedral in their city. They might see Mother Angelica on their television sets or cheer for Notre Dame on Saturday afternoons in autumn. They might visit Catholic cathedrals in European cities or admire church steeples off in the distance as they approach small towns in Quebec. They might see on their neighbor's lawn a statue of Mary, Christ's mother, or of St. Francis with a bird resting on his welcoming outstretched hand. The presence of Catholics and signs of their beliefs are visible in many forms.

Less often do people realize that the Roman Catholic Church also has other branches, made up of the Eastern Catholic Churches. Eastern Catholic Churches have their own spiritual leaders, called "patriarchs", but they also recognize the pope, the leader of the Roman Catholic Church, as their spiritual leader. These Eastern branches of the Roman Catholic Church, however, have their roots in the Eastern Orthodox Churches and, thus, in the Eastern wing of the ancient Roman Empire. As we will see in our discussion of the history of these Churches, the Eastern Rite of the Roman Catholic Church is strongly connected with the practices and traditions of the Eastern Orthodox Churches that separated from Rome in 1054. They are, generally, former Eastern Orthodox Churches that have returned to union with Rome.

The Eastern Orthodox Churches are the Christian Churches connected to the ancient Eastern Roman Empire. The most famous political and religious centers of this empire were the ancient cities of Constantinople, Alexandria, Antioch, and Jerusalem. The bishops of these cities were considered patriarchs, since they were the bishops who ruled over all the other bishops of the region. They were given special honor and respect. Rome, considered the oldest and primary diocese, held a primacy of honor above all the rest. Due to the various disputes over doctrine and authority, all these Eastern patriarchates eventually separated from Rome. These are the Eastern Orthodox Churches. Subsequently, sizeable portions of these Churches reunited with Rome. These are the Eastern Catholic Churches.

Eastern Catholics are Catholics, and when there is a discussion of Catholic beliefs in this volume, the discussion includes the beliefs of both Western and Eastern Catholics. When, however, certain ceremonies or legal traditions in the Eastern Catholic Churches (often parallel to practices in the Eastern Orthodox Churches) differ from the Western Roman Catholic tradition, we will note these variations. The Eastern Orthodox Churches have a few doctrinal differences from the Western or Eastern Rite Catholic Churches, and we will point them out in the discussion of the basic beliefs of these various communities.

■ *St. Patrick's Cathedral with its neo-Gothic spires, nestled amid the skyscrapers of Manhattan in New York City.*

Catholic Churches in America

The lives of Americans have been influenced by Catholics in many ways. Catholic schools in America have educated millions of citizens, and Catholic hospitals have cared for millions of patients. Catholic charities have served the poor and sheltered the homeless. With other Christian Churches, the Catholic Church has celebrated America's most festive holiday,

Christmas. It has also added particular Catholic celebrations: Saint Patrick's Day in Irish neighborhoods; Saint Anthony's Feast in Italian districts; Saint Barbara's Feast in Eastern Catholic parishes with links to the Near East; and Saint Lazarus Saturday, with its processions in Syrian and Lebanese communities on the eve of Palm Sunday. Catholics have served in the military at all ranks and in state and national senates and houses of representatives. John F. Kennedy was the first Catholic president. In all facets of American life, Catholics have played a large part. They have also brought a great deal of diversity to American life. If you drive around American cities, you might find Roman Catholic churches named after Saint Ludwig (German), Saint Brendan (Irish), Saint Louis (French), Saint Stephen (Hungarian), Saint Theresa of Avila (Spanish), Saint Bartholomew (Armenian), or Saint Charbel (Maronites, especially from Lebanon).

Orthodox Churches in America

The first Orthodox Church on the American continent was established in 1792 by eight monks from western Russia on Kodiak Island, in present-day Alaska. The Russian Orthodox Church is unique among major religious groups in America: it is the only church to expand from West to East. It moved its original headquarters from Sitka, Alaska to San Francisco, then to New York City. The Church of Saint Nicholas, built in 1901 in New York City, became the main Russian Orthodox Church in America in 1905. There were at that time about 20,000 members in 60 parishes throughout America, but within a decade the numbers had grown to 100,000 with 169 parishes, and by 1975 there were more than a million parishioners. The Greek Orthodox Church established itself toward the end of the 19th century in the large cities of New York and Chicago and fanned out to other regions, numbering more than two million in 1975, the largest representative of Eastern Orthodoxy in the Western world. Today, estimates indicate that there are more than 3 million members of the Orthodox Church of America, which is the name of the church that formerly was called the Russian Orthodox Greek Catholic Church of America. Other ethnic groups of Eastern Orthodox Christians (Albanians, Bulgarians,

Romanians, Serbians, Syrians, and Ukrainians) arrived in the 20th century. Many of the Orthodox Churches keep strong ties, at least in tradition and spirit, with their respective mother churches and train their clergy there.

Eastern Church Visibility

Eastern Churches, both Orthodox and Catholic, are less familiar to many Americans, since their numbers are smaller and their locations are limited to certain cities or regions of the country. However, events at times bring their presence into full view. Pope John Paul II's visit to Romania in June, 2001, for example, brought attention to the religious complexity of the Eastern Churches in that country. The vast majority of Christians are Orthodox. Still, there are over a million believers who belong to the Romanian Greek Catholic Church that is united with Rome. Of the Orthodox, a large portion are under the jurisdiction of the patriarchate of Moscow, while others are striving to establish an independent Romanian Church. Further, during the Second World War, General Joseph Stalin of Russia confiscated the property of the Romanian Greek Catholic Church and gave it to the Orthodox who were linked to Moscow. A papal visit, then, raises issues of religious jurisdiction and property rights that are very complex and difficult to understand.

Catholic Diversity and Unity

The Catholic Church in America is a "melting pot" like America itself. Its members are not all descendants of Western European countries. They come also from Africa, Asia, Australia, and South and Central America. Others (for example, Eastern Rite Catholics), in smaller numbers, come from Eastern Europe. They bring all their own varied traditions. Yet, the hierarchical structure of the Catholic Church, while allowing room for diversity, tends to produce a strong unity of belief and practice. Religious celebrations may vary in terms of the types of music, such as Gregorian chant in a Catholic monastery or guitar-led hymns in a university chapel, but the ritual of a Catholic Mass remains essentially fixed throughout the whole Catholic world. If American Catholics were to travel to Saint Mark's Basilica in

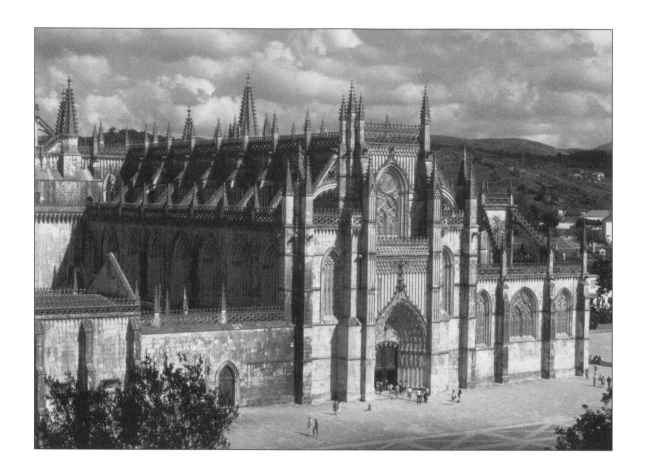

■ *The former Dominican monastery of Maria da Victoria was built during the 15th century in the tiny town of Batalha, Portugal.*

Venice or Saint Vitus's Cathedral in Prague, despite the language differences, they would feel at home: the basic structure of the Mass would be familiar. With the central authority of the pope and bishops, and required church approval of religious teachings and practices, the Catholic Church tends to preserve a bond of unified faith among its members throughout the world.

Orthodox Diversity and Unity

The general tendency in Eastern Orthodox Churches is toward independence. The early Eastern Churches before the break-up with Rome always insisted on independent jurisdictions despite the primacy of honor that was accorded to Rome. This independent spirit has tended to show itself in the more national identity of the various Orthodox Churches (Russian, Greek, Albanian, Bulgarian, etc.). The agreement in basic Christian doctrines and the uniform structure of the Divine Liturgy binds these Churches to a common tradition of faith. Their diversity is often due to the limitation of each church's ministry to its own ethnic heritage.

The Meaning of "Catholic"

The word *catholic* comes from the Greek word meaning "universal." "Go, teach all nations," was the command that Jesus Christ gave to his apostles. Although Catholics have their roots in Judaism, since Jesus was a Jew and so were his first followers, Catholicism is a religion open to all people. The Gospel of Jesus, as viewed by Catholics, is not a simple replacement for the Jewish Scriptures. It is a fulfillment of what the Jewish Scriptures promised. In the 5th chapter of Matthew's Gospel, Jesus Christ says:

> *Do not think that I have come to abolish the law or the prophets; I have come not to abolish but to fulfill. For truly I tell you, until heaven and earth pass away, not one letter, not one stroke of a letter, will pass from the law until all is accomplished.* (Matt. 5.17)

The Meaning of "Orthodox"

The word *orthodox* comes from the Greek *orthos,* meaning "right" or "correct," and *doxa,* meaning "belief" or "teaching." Originally, the phrase *orthodox church,* was used to indicate all the Christian Churches that held to the teachings determined in the early Christian Church as correct, in contrast to heretical teachings. In the ancient historical context, it signified the teachings of the Roman and Eastern Churches that held the correct belief concerning the doctrine of the Trinity and the identity of Jesus Christ as one person who is both God and man, in contrast to the heretical teachings of the Nestorians and the Monophysites. Nestorius and his followers claimed that there were two persons in Christ and that it was only the human person of Christ that was born of Mary and died on the Cross. They thus denied the orthodox, or correct, teaching that Christ was one person who united in himself both a divine and human nature. The Monophysites taught that there was only one nature, a divine nature, in Christ. The teachings of both Rome and the Churches of the East that were not heretical were thus called "orthodox." At first, then, it was a term applied to Western and Eastern Churches who ageed with the teachings of the early ecumenical, or general, councils of the Church. Only later did the term *Eastern Orthodox* or *Orthodox* come to be attached to the Eastern Churches who separated from Rome in the 11th century.

The Christian View of "Old Law, New Law"

From the perspective of Catholics and Eastern Orthodox Christians, God's chosen people before Jesus Christ were a particular people, the Jewish people. According to God's plan, revealed in the Old Testament Scriptures, the Jews were, by their dedication to God's law and by their religious example, meant to influence other peoples and lead them to God. According to the Jewish law and the prophets, even as God's special people, they were meant by God to spread the message of divine care or concern for all peoples of the world to their neighbors. Despite this calling to influence "the nations," they often kept themselves apart from others by their special Jewish customs and ceremonies. Jesus Christ, however, by his interpretation of the Old Law and presentation of the New Law, released his followers from many of these specifically Jewish rituals that set Jews apart. In the Catholic and Orthodox view, he took the letter of the Jewish law and gave it a spiritual interpretation that made it more universal.

As Saint Paul argues in his Letter to the Galatians:

Before faith came, we were held in custody under law,
confined for the faith that was to be revealed.
Consequently, the law was our disciplinarian for Christ,
that we might be justified by faith. But now that faith
has come, we are no longer under a disciplinarian.
For through faith you are all children of God in Christ
Jesus. For all of you who were baptized into Christ have
clothed yourselves with Christ. There is neither Jew nor

Greek, there is neither slave nor free person, there is not male and female, for you are all one in Christ Jesus. And if you belong to Christ, then you are Abraham's descendant, heirs according to the promise.
(Gal. 3.23–29)

Jesus Christ thus extended the New Law to a world beyond the Jewish people. It is this universal spiritual law that one of his disciples, Saint Paul, carried to the world outside of Palestine—to the people to whom he writes in his Epistles or Letters: the Galatians, the Ephesians, the Colossians, the Corinthians, and the Romans. The spreading of Christ's teachings beyond these cities to the whole world has taken many centuries. In the Far East and in Muslim territories, its influence is still very small. Of the roughly five billion people in the world, however, approximately one and a half billion are Catholics. About 215 million more are Orthodox Christians.

Preaching the Gospel to All Nations

The universal extension of the Catholic Church may be seen in the large crowds that gather for Pope John Paul II's many trips to South America, Africa, Asia, the Near East, and Eastern Europe. It can be noticed in the large percentage of Catholics throughout the world: Mexico (95 percent), Argentina (90 percent), the Philippines (85 percent), Poland (95 percent), and the United States (26 percent). On a more grand scale, the universal drive of the Catholic Church can be discovered in the growing numbers of Catholics in Africa.

Although the Catholic Church is viewed by most people as a Western Church anchored in Rome, this does not give a completely accurate picture. As we have said, there are many Eastern Rite Catholic Churches that once were separated from the Roman Church but which, over centuries, have returned to union with Rome. Thus, in the United States and abroad, Romanian Catholics, Ukrainian Catholics, Armenian Catholics, Melkite Catholics, and many other forms of Eastern Catholics, are united in faith with the large number of Roman Catholics of Western background.

A volunteer chef pouring soup for the needy in the kitchen of St. Francis Xavier Church in New York City.

Of the approximately 215 million Eastern Orthodox Christians, the largest numbers are found in the Greek and Russian Orthodox Churches. Three-quarters of the world's Orthodox Christians are Europeans. The next largest group, about 15 percent, is found in Africa. Asia, especially the Near East, has about 7 percent of the Orthodox population. The United States and Canada now claim about five million Orthodox Christians, whereas South America numbers a little over half a million members.

The Church's Mission

Christ gave to his Church a mission that it would seek the return of all humanity and all aspects of human life to his Father in heaven. For Catholics and Orthodox Christians, Christ continues to live in the Church and its members, and through him the Church has the power and guidance to teach and to promote the spiritual life of his followers.

Every aspect of a Christian's life is linked to Christ. Christians attempt to imitate the devotion Christ had to always follow His Father's will. Saint Paul often speaks of the members of the Church as the body of Christ and of Christ himself as the Head of the Church. The Church gets its universality from its

Head, Jesus Christ, and its mission is to bring Christ's helping grace to all creation. That is why its members are called to redeem all things. In their attempts to accomplish this mission, they are called to help people in need and to comfort, forgive, and bear wrongs patiently.

The "Works of Mercy"

These "works of mercy," both physical and spiritual, summarize the words spoken by Christ himself in chapter 25 of Matthew's Gospel:

> *Come, you that are blessed by my Father, inherit the kingdom prepared for you from the foundation of the world: for I was hungry and you gave me food, I was thirsty and you gave me something to drink, I was a stranger and you welcomed me, I was naked and you gave me clothing. I was sick and you took care of me, I was in prison and you visited me. Then the righteous will answer him, 'Lord, when was it that we saw you hungry and gave you food, or thirsty and gave you something to drink?'... And the king will answer them, 'Truly I tell you, just as you did it to one of the least of these who are members of my family, you did it to me.'*
> (Matt. 25.34–40)

This is why it is not strange to visit a sick relative at a hospital with a name like Saint Luke's or Saint Jude's. Neither is it unexpected that lodging for the homeless will be found in hospices supported by Catholic and Orthodox Churches. Nor is it surprising to see the Eucharist from a Catholic Mass or an Orthodox Divine Liturgy being brought to the homebound sick. These are the ordinary actions that show Christians' efforts to bring the teachings of Christ to all.

There are also the extraordinary efforts of dedicated Catholics around the world. Mother Teresa and her followers are famous in all nations for their dedication to the poor and the sick of Calcutta and many other cities. Today, especially in Europe, there are many Roman Catholic lay communities who combine an ordinary life in the world with regular communal prayer and service to the poor. In the Middle East, Father Elias Chacour, an Arab Eastern Catholic priest, is known for his efforts to bring about non-violent cooperation and understanding between Palestinians and Israelis. In Russia, a recent Russian Orthodox martyr is Father Alexander Men (1935–1990), a popular priest known for his holiness and dynamic preaching. He proclaimed the Christian message boldly even while under constant KGB, or Secret Police, surveillance and intimidation. He was struck by an axe and killed on September 9, 1990.

In almost every city and town in America ordinary examples of the works of mercy are visible today. They have become traditional. Many of the missions American Catholics and Orthodox assign to churches and church institutions are part of what they inherited from Eastern and Western Europe, Africa, South America, and Canada. Their many welcoming practices and festive celebrations were and are ways of feeding the hungry, clothing the naked, and welcoming the strangers from foreign lands.

- When Germans or Italians arrived in America in the late 19th or early 20th centuries, they discovered Catholic churches founded by their predecessors that made them feel at home. Religious services, then in Latin, were the same as in their homeland, and so were the hymns, often sung in their native tongues. Celebrations of the feast of Saint Anthony in the North End of Boston, on Mott Street in New York City, and on the streets of Cassino, Italy, have remarkable similarities that bring warmth and comfort to the hearts of Italian Catholics.

- The blessing of the Portuguese fishing fleet would be as familiar to the people of Gloucester, Massachusetts, and Newport Beach, California, as to those of Lisbon or Oporto in Portugal or of Vitoria or Santos in Brazil.

- French Canadians who poured into New England in the latter part of the 19th century brought with them their language and celebrations. A New England

Catholic of French Canadian background would feel quite at home at the Church of Notre Dame in Montreal or at the shrine of Saint Anne de Beaupré, just outside of Quebec, or in a small town church in the rural villages of Northern Maine or Vermont.

- Many Eastern Orthodox and Eastern Catholic Churches have held annual national conferences in different regions of the United States to teach their faithful the various aspects of their spiritual traditions, to celebrate the Divine Liturgy, to preserve their ethnic heritage, and to welcome new arrivals. Their Christian faith links them to Christ and to their native lands and helps them build new lives in their new homeland.

In the name of Christ, Catholics and Orthodox Christians in these ordinary situations made their fellow countrymen feel at home. Many of these welcoming practices survive today and have been extended to new arrivals from the Spanish-speaking countries of Central and South America, to the French-speaking Haitians, to Catholic immigrants from Southeast Asia, and to the Catholics and Orthodox from Eastern Europe and the Near East.

These diverse activities of Catholic and Orthodox religious and lay people show the continuing presence of Christ in his Church. When Jesus told his followers to "go and make disciples of all nations," he added the words: "and remember, I am with you always, to the end of the age." (Matt. 28.19–20). Catholics and Orthodox believe that Christ acts through them as his instruments. As creatures of a loving God, they have their God-given natural abilities. As instruments of Christ's mission to bring salvation to the whole world, they believe that Christ acts through them when they feed the hungry, comfort the troubled, visit the bedridden, welcome a stranger, or heal the sick.

The Commitment to Education

Realizing that the American public schools could not foster any particular religious beliefs, Catholics decided to build their own schools. As necessity demanded, they built elementary schools, high schools, colleges, and universities.

This strong commitment to education is not new, and follows from the awareness that Catholics, along with many others, have of its importance. In the 16th, 17th, and 18th centuries in Italy and France, a large number of religious communities of women were formed that were dedicated to education. They have continued to carry out their work of educating the young throughout Europe, as well as in the many primary and secondary religious schools they founded in the United States and Canada.

The Eastern Orthodox, when their numbers could support them, also built parish schools, colleges, and seminaries to train their faithful, their teachers, and their priests. This is especially the case with the Greek Orthodox who have established Hellenic College and the Holy Cross Greek Orthodox Theological School in Boston. St. Vladimir's Seminary in Westwood, NY, under the auspices of the Orthodox Church of America, is one of the most prestigious seminaries in the world. These institutions continue a long educational tradition of the Eastern Churches.

The early Christian writers of the East and West realized the importance of eductation. Saints Basil and Gregory of Nyssa from the East, and Saints Jerome and Augustine from the West, argued that Christians could only defend themselves against opponents if they were good at rhetoric, and they could explain their faith coherently and intelligently only if there were adept at logic. Saint Augustine in the 5th century particularly urged Christians to pursue any studies "by which our most wholesome faith, which leads to eternal life, may be begotten, nourished, strengthened, and defended." (*On the Trinity*, XIV, 1) He thus gave the basic justification for the future of all levels of Christian education.

The Way of Life

For Catholics, as well as for Eastern Orthodox Christians, all these works of mercy that show Christ's enduring presence in today's world only have merit if they are performed in union with Christ. This common vision of the role of Christ in Catholic and Eastern Orthodox life is well-expressed in *The Catechism of the Catholic Church:*

Christ is always present in his Church, especially in her liturgical celebrations. He is present in the Sacrifice of the Mass [or Divine Liturgy] not only in the person of his minister, 'the same now offering, through the ministry of priests, who formerly offered himself on the cross,' but especially in the Eucharistic species. By his power he is present in the sacraments so that when anybody baptizes, it is really Christ himself who baptizes. He is present in his word since it is he himself who speaks when the holy Scriptures are read in the Church. Lastly, he is present when the Church prays and sings, for he has promised 'where two or three are gathered together in my name there am I in the midst of them.'
 (1088)

Catholics and Orthodox Christians believe that the ideas expressed in this declaration hold not only for official religious celebrations; they hold for all good works. It is Christ who works through believers as they reach out to their neighbors. He teaches when they teach. He forgives when they forgive. He heals when they care for the sick. He reaches out when they extend a helping hand. He blesses when they embrace the suffering and the oppressed.

CHAPTER 2

The Origins of the Catholic and Orthodox Churches

A simple description of the origins of the Christian Church might begin with the portrait of Christ, its founder, telling his disciple Peter: "You are Peter, and on this rock I will build my church." (Matt. 16.18) Catholic and Eastern Orthodox believers, however, view the Church as part of God's involvement with people long before this event. The Church is, thus, part of the whole of the history of God's dealings with mankind. To discover the deeper roots of the Church, then, it would be helpful to know something of the prior Jewish tradition upon which Christianity was built.

Christians speak of the Jewish people's religious history as the Old Testament. They describe the Ten Commandments, and all the laws found in the Jewish Scriptures, as the Old Law. They refer to the agreement between God and his chosen people—a pact whereby God would watch over the Jews in a special way and they, on their part, would obey his commandments—as the Old Covenant. In contrast, in speaking of their own religious association with God, Catholics and Orthodox Christians, like all Christians, speak of the New Testament, the New Law, and the New Covenant.

To speak of a new covenant implies one of two things: either that God has totally rejected his previous covenant, or he is continuing his original covenant but doing so in a different way. Christians portray the New Covenant as a continuation of the Old Covenant. The Old Law continues in its moral demands, so that the Ten Commandments, which we will discuss later, still must be observed in the New Law. Yet, many of the Old Testament observances are set aside: Christ's sacrifice, for example, replaces all the animal sacrifices required by the Old Law, since Christ's death, as the death of the Son of God, is worth more than any creature's sacrifice.

Continuity and Discontinuity

Since the Church is the community that continues the covenant God made with his chosen people, many of the images of the Old Covenant or Old Testament carry over into the New Covenant or Testament. The Church continues to be the community of God's people, those whom he chose to make his special people. One of the descriptions of the Church, then, is "the people of God." "People of God" is an image taken from the Old Testament. It is an image that is worth examining to appreciate the new meaning that was given to it in the New Testament. It is an image that begins with the story of Abraham.

Abraham

In the opening book of the Bible, Genesis, Abraham is introduced. It is with him especially that the Christian story of God's covenant with men begins:

> *I will make you exceedingly fruitful; and I will make nations of you, and kings shall come from you. I will establish my covenant between me and you, and your offspring after you throughout their generations, for an everlasting covenant, to be God to you and to your offspring after you. And I will give to you, and to your offspring after you, the land where you are now an alien, all the land of Canaan, for a perpetual holding; and I will be their God.* (Gen. 17.6–8)

God thereby made a covenant with Abraham and his off-spring. They would be his special people and he would be their God. For Catholics and Orthodox Christians, this covenant with Abraham would tell them something about their own New Covenant with God. They would be God's new special people and he would be their God. Their new inheritance as children of God did not totally negate the Old Covenant. It did not free them from the moral obligations of the Old Law:

> I am the Lord your God, who brought you out of the land of Egypt, out of the house of slavery; you shall have no other gods before me. You shall not make for yourself an idol, whether in the form of anything that is in heaven above, or that is on the earth beneath, or that is in the water under the earth. You shall not bow down to them or worship them; for I the Lord your God am a jealous God, punishing children for iniquity of parents, to the third and fourth generation of those who reject me, but showing steadfast love to the thousandth generation of those who love me and keep my commandments. You shall not make wrongful use of the name of the Lord your God, for the Lord will not acquit anyone who misuses his name. Remember the Sabbath day, and keep it holy....Honor your father and your mother, so that your days may be long in the land that the Lord your God is giving you. You shall not murder. You shall not commit adultery. You shall not steal. You shall not bear false witness against your neighbor. You shall not covet your neighbor's house; you shall not covet your neighbor's wife, or male or female slave, or ox, or donkey, or anything that belongs to your neighbor. (Ex. 20.2–17)

These commandments of the Old Law remained as requirements of the New Law. In this way, the New Law continues the Old Law.

The Coming Messiah

The frequent domination of the Jewish people by many more powerful nations inspired a hope for a new leader, who might free them from their oppressors. In the years before Jesus Christ's birth, prophets foretold the coming of a Messiah who would save God's people and establish the kingdom promised to Abraham. This Messiah was pictured in different ways by Jewish writers: some imagined him as a military leader overthrowing their oppressors; others expected him to be a great teacher; still others, more rarely, thought of him as a suffering servant.

Matthew's Gospel introduces Jesus Christ with the following words: "An account of the genealogy of Jesus the Messiah, the son of David, the son of Abraham." (Matt. 1.1) Jesus is thus presented as the offspring of Abraham from whom a great nation would descend. He is also, like David, a king who can lead his people.

The opening words of this Gospel, then, recall the long-held hopes of the sons of Abraham and the Jewish people who had been suppressed for so many centuries. It was during these days of high expectations for a Messiah that Jesus began to preach among the Jewish people.

Some saw this wandering preacher as merely another rabbi or teacher who spent his days interpreting and reshaping Jewish law. Others saw him as a leader in their fight against Roman rule. Still others saw him as the Messiah, sent by God to deliver them.

The principal source of information about his life is the New Testament of the Christian Bible, especially the Gospels of Matthew, Mark, Luke, and John. Stories about the life and deeds of Jesus Christ and what he taught circulated first by word of mouth. Later, they were collected and written down. It was from such oral and written sources that the Gospels of the four evangelists were compiled. The first of these, the Gospel of Mark, was written about 62, only thirty years after the death of Jesus. Written so soon after the events they describe, these books present a strong body of evidence for the existence of Jesus and the content of his preaching.

The Gospel Account of Jesus' Youth

The Gospels tell little about the childhood of Jesus. Following the customs of the time, he most likely began to work alongside his earthly father, Joseph, learning the trade of carpenter. Probably he followed the ritual observances of the Jewish law and studied the Old Testament stories. Luke's Gospel tells us that when Jesus was twelve years old, he went with his mother Mary and with Joseph to Jerusalem to celebrate the Passover. Unknown to Mary and Joseph, he stayed behind as the caravan headed back to Nazareth. When they discovered that he was missing, they went back to Jerusalem. "They found him in the temple, sitting among the teachers, listening to them and asking them questions." (Luke 2.46)

When Jesus was about thirty years old, a preacher called John the Baptist began a new religious movement. He announced to the people the coming of the Messiah (the Anointed One) and urged them to prepare for his arrival by repenting of their sins. John used flowing water as a sign of washing away their sins. And so before he preached, John baptized people by immersing them in the water of the River Jordan. Jesus was one of the many who went to John to be baptized. According to the Gospel of Mark (1.7–8), John proclaimed: "The one who is more powerful than I is coming after me; I am not worthy to stoop down and untie the thong of his sandals. I have baptized you with water; but he will baptize you with the Holy Spirit."

Following John's arrest and imprisonment, Jesus began his own ministry, preaching repentance and telling his listeners "to believe in the good news": that the kingdom of God or the kingdom of heaven is near. The "gospel," or the "good news," that Jesus taught in his sermons and stories was new. Yet, he insisted that he was not setting aside the Old Law, but was extending and enriching it.

Jesus as the New Lawgiver

In chapter 5 of his Gospel, Matthew tells about Jesus' Sermon on the Mount. This sermon sets up many parallels with Moses' reception of the Ten Commandments of the Old Law. First of all, like Moses' reception of the Ten Commandments, it takes place on a mountain. Next, it sets a deliberately different tone than the "Thou shalt nots" of the Old Testament code:

■ **The Twelve Apostles of Christ**

Peter

Andrew

James,
 the son of Zebedee

John

Philip

Bartholomew

Thomas

Matthew,
 the tax collector

James,
 the son of Alphaeus

Thaddaeus

Simon,
 the Cananean

Judas Iscariot
 –(Matt. 10.2–4)

*Blessed are the poor in spirit, for theirs is the kingdom
of heaven. Blessed are those who mourn, for they shall
be comforted. Blessed are the meek, for they shall inherit
the earth. Blessed are those who hunger and thirst for
righteousness, for they shall be satisfied. Blessed are the
merciful, for they shall obtain mercy. Blessed are the
pure in heart, for they shall see God. Blessed are the
peacemakers, for they shall be called sons of God.
Blessed are those who are persecuted for righteousness'
sake, for theirs is the kingdom of heaven.* (Matt. 5.3–10)

Moreover, according to Matthew's account, Moses had
received the Old Law from God; Jesus proclaims the New Law
as God:

*You have heard that it was said to those of ancient
times, 'You shall not murder'; and 'Whoever murders
shall be liable to judgment.' But I say to you that if you
are angry with a brother or sister, you will be liable to
judgment; and if you insult a brother or sister, you will
be liable to the council; and if you say, 'You fool,' you
will be liable to the hell of fire.* (Matt. 5.21–22)

In Matthew's Gospel, Jesus speaks as a lawgiver—that is,
he speaks with divine authority.

The scribes and Pharisees, experts in the interpretation of
the Old Testament Law, challenged Jesus' teachings concerning
the New Law and his interpretation of the texts of the Old Law.
On many occasions they tried to entrap Jesus with their questions. Jesus, however, defended himself and justified his interpretation of the Old Law. As Matthew indicates: "And from that
day on no one dared to ask him any more questions." (Matt. 22.46)

Jesus as Suffering Servant

Jesus' preaching had made him well-known. When he traveled from Galilee to Jerusalem for Passover, his entry into the
city was triumphal. According to Matthew's Gospel (21.8–11),
crowds of people were proclaiming him the Messiah. In the traditional Eastern manner, many honored him by throwing their

cloaks in front of him, and others cut branches from trees and spread them in his path.

However, when Jesus' presence in Jerusalem became known to the priests of the temple and to the Pharisees and scribes, these teachers and lawyers began to plot against him. These religious leaders attacked Jesus for his disregard of the legal and ceremonial aspects of Jewish laws and for his preaching of spiritual and moral reform.

When Jesus arrived at the temple he assailed the irreverence that he found there. Instead of a holy place, he found it to be a noisy bazaar. They were selling doves and animals to be offered as sacrifices and shouting out the rates of money exchange. He overturned the tables of the money changers and the seats of those who sold doves and said to them: "It is written, 'My house shall be called a house of prayer,' but you are making it a den of robbers." (Matt. 21.13) The chief priests and scribes challenged him, asking, "By what authority are you doing these things, and who gave you this authority?" (Matt. 21.23) Jesus sensed the danger such questions implied and the growing anger of the scribes, the Pharisees, and the chief priests against him.

The Last Supper

For Passover, a major feast celebrating the release of the Jews from Egyptian slavery, Jesus and his twelve disciples gathered in the house of one of his followers to have supper together. To teach his disciples an important lesson, Jesus washed his disciples' feet, saying to them, "Now I have set you an example, that you should do as I have done. Very truly I tell you, servants are not greater than their master; nor are messengers greater than the one who sent them." (John 13.15–16)

During this Passover meal Jesus spoke the words that are the foundation for the Catholic and Orthodox sacrament of the Eucharist. They believe that the bread and wine at the last supper was changed by Jesus into his body and blood. "While they were eating, Jesus took a loaf of bread, and after blessing it he broke it, gave it to the disciples, and said, 'Take, eat; this is my body.' Then he took a cup, and after giving thanks he gave it to them, saying, 'Drink from it, all of you, for this is my blood of the

Leonardo da Vinci's recently restored **The Last Supper,** portraying Jesus Christ's celebration of the Passover with his apostles.

covenant, which is poured out for many for the forgiveness of sins." (Matt. 26.26–28)

It was also during this meal that Jesus revealed that he would be betrayed by one of his disciples: "Truly, I tell you, one of you will betray me." (Matt. 26.21) Judas left the room.

Jesus' departing words as they left supper were:

Little children, I am with you only a little longer. You will look for me; and as I said to the Jews so now I say to you, 'Where I am going, you cannot come.' I give you a new commandment, that you love one another. Just as I have loved you, you also should love one another. By this everyone will know that you are my disciples, if you have love for one another. (John 13.33–35)

Jesus' Crucifixion and Death

The Gospels tell of Jesus' last days. After the Last Supper, Jesus went to a garden called Gethsemane. There he often went for prayer. On that night, the disciples went with him. As his disciples slept around him, the prayerful silence of the garden was broken by the arrival of Judas, leading a band of soldiers. Jesus was arrested and brought before the Sanhedrin, or council of Jewish leaders. They found Jesus guilty of calling himself the Son of God. However, Roman Law prevented them from putting him to death on the basis of their own laws. To ensure his death, they brought him before Pontius Pilate, the Roman official, and charged him not only with blasphemy but also with organizing a revolt against Rome. Despite his hesitancy, Pilate gave in to the Jewish leaders and sentenced him to death by crucifixion.

Crucifixion was the form of death reserved by the Romans for thieves and revolutionaries. Matthew, however, in his Gospel (Matt. 8.17), sees Jesus' sufferings as the fulfillment of Isaiah's prophecy that the Messiah would be a suffering servant:

He was despised and rejected by others; a man of suffering and acquainted with infirmity; and as one from whom others hide their faces he was despised, and we held him of no account. Surely he has borne our infirmities and carried our diseases; yet we accounted him stricken, struck down by God, and afflicted. But he was wounded for our transgressions, crushed for our iniquities; upon him was the punishment that made us whole, and by his bruises we are healed. (Isaiah 53.3–5)

Pontius Pilate ordered a sign nailed to Jesus' cross to mock the Jews who did not acknowledge him as the Messiah: "Jesus of Nazareth, King of the Jews," it said in Aramaic, Greek, and Latin (John 19.19–20). That is why many crosses today carry the initials "INRI," which is the abbreviation for the Latin version of this phrase.

As the soldiers and the mob taunted the dying Jesus, he prayed: "Father, forgive them for they know not what they do." (Luke 23.34) Finally, after hours of unbearable pain, he cried out, "My God, my God, why hast thou forsaken me?" (Matt. 27.46). Then he expired.

The Gospel of Matthew reports the main witnesses:

Many women were also there, looking on from a distance; they had followed Jesus from Galilee and had provided for him. Among them were Mary Magdalene,

■ The **Crucifixion**, painted by Piero della Francesca, shows the final hours of Christ's life. The crucifixion scene is recounted in each of the four gospels (Matthew, Mark, Luke, and John).

and Mary the mother of James and Joseph, and the mother of the sons of Zebedee.
  (Matthew 27.55–56, Mark 15.40–41, Luke 23.49)

A Roman officer reported to Pilate that Jesus was dead. Christ's body was turned over to one of his followers, Joseph of Arimathea, for burial. It was wrapped in a linen shroud and placed in a tomb that was sealed with a large rock.

The Resurrection of Jesus

According to Matthew's Gospel, on the third day after Jesus was crucified, Mary Magdalene and Mary, the mother of James and Joseph, went to see the sepulchre, the tomb in a cave where Jesus was buried. But Jesus was not there. An angel had descended from heaven and rolled back the stone. He told the women: "Do not be afraid; I know that you are looking for Jesus who was crucified…. He has been raised from the dead." (Matt. 28.2–6)

Later, according to the Gospel, Christ appeared to the eleven disciples and commissioned them to preach the gospel and baptize:

> *All authority in heaven and on earth has been given to me. Go therefore and make disciples of all nations, baptizing them in the name of the Father, and of the Son and of the Holy Spirit, teaching them to observe all that I have commanded you; and lo, I am with you always to the close of the age.* (Matt. 28.18–20)

With these words, the story of Jesus according to Matthew's Gospel ends. Yet, according to Christian belief, Christ himself continued, and continues, to live through his Church.

The Christian View of Biblical History

For Catholics and Orthodox Christians, the biblical stories are not just recollections of historical happenings. They manifest God's involvement with his chosen people and the lessons he wanted to teach them by the various events of his providential care. To understand Christ and his Church, it is necessary to appreciate as well as possible God's whole involvement with humankind. Each event of biblical history sheds light on the other events of the story. They tell something of God's plan for all of creation. The story of Abraham tells something about Christ. Moses' commandments tell something about the Sermon on the Mount. The Jews' escape from the slavery of Egypt tells something about the escape of all men from the slavery of sin. The sacrifice of a lamb in the Jerusalem temple tells about the sacrifice of Christ, the Lamb of God, on the Cross. Each part of the biblical story tells something about the other parts. This is why the story of the origin of the Church needs the whole of the Old and New Testaments to show how the Church fits into the whole of God's plan for man's redemption and the role of the Church in it.

CHAPTER 3

The History of the Catholic and Orthodox Churches

*A*ccording to Catholic and Orthodox belief, it was forty days after Jesus Christ's resurrection from the dead that he ascended into heaven. According to the Acts of the Apostles, Christ's ascension left his disciples lonely and confused. As they huddled together in fear and bewilderment, the Acts of the Apostles reports that:

> *Suddenly from heaven there came a sound like a violent wind, and it filled the entire house where they were sitting. Divided tongues, as of fire, appeared among them, and a tongue rested on each of them. All of them were filled with the Holy Spirit and began to speak in other languages, as the Spirit gave them ability.* (Acts 2.2–4)

Thereafter, according to the Christian Scriptures, the apostles gained courage and became missionaries, fulfilling the final directive of their risen and ascended Lord: "Go therefore and make disciples of all nations, baptizing them in the name of the Father and of the Son and of the Holy Spirit." (Matt. 28.19) They went about teaching the main Christian message: that Jesus was the true son promised to Abraham, that he was the Messiah, that

he was the Son of God who became man, that he was crucified and raised from the dead, and that through him sins are forgiven and eternal salvation is offered to all people.

The Early Christian Church

The first Christians were the disciples of Christ, the simple fishermen who followed him. The first Christian "church" was the Jewish community that had heard Jesus preach, watched the wonders he performed, and saw in him a great prophet and then more than a prophet. The early origins of the Christian Church are hardly distinguishable from a special Jewish community. Many Jews saw Christ as a special rabbi, a special teacher. Only gradually did they come to believe that Christ was more than just a teacher and that he had a larger mission. At first, they continued to perform all the Jewish rituals on the Sabbath. Little by little they reenacted the Passover meal with its new meaning, realizing that Christ had, by his death and resurrection, given it a new reality. As the fuller meaning of Christ's life and teaching dawned on them, Christian historians tell us, they began to separate from the temple and synagogue. It is this stage of development that is chronicled in the Gospel of Matthew, at times called "the gospel of the Jewish Christian community."

Christians believe that Christ was a teacher, but one who gave a New Law in his own name, thereby indicating that he was God. When he spoke of God as his Father, he spoke, according to Christian believers, as one equal to his Father. They believe that his teachings gave a whole new meaning to the Old Law, and his death was a sacrifice that replaced all the sacrifices of the Old Law. His resurrection, according to Christian faith, was a guarantee of his claims and of his promises. These claims also called for believers to have the same kind of unwavering faith in God as Abraham had. Christ called not just for obedience to a law; he called for a new faith that believed the new meanings and the new vision he brought to human life. These themes of the Jewish community of Christians, sounded in Matthew's Gospel, also are the themes of the Epistle to the Hebrews. Both these writings put us in touch with the first community of Christians—the Jewish community of Christians.

The Gospel Preached to the Gentiles

Paul, a key writer of the New Testament who was martyred in 64, may have preached to the Hebrews, but it is not for that work that he is best known. As he says in his Letter to the Galatians, a Gentile (non-Jewish) people to whom he had preached about Christ, he had been a very fervent Jew. He studied under the great Rabbi Gamaliel. He even persecuted the Christians and was present at the death of the first Christian martyr, Stephen. However, God brought him to a dramatic conversion. Thus, Saul of Tarsus became Paul, the Apostle to the Gentiles. His letters to the many Christian communities show a man of tireless energy and daring adventures. His journeys are recounted in the Acts of the Apostles, chapters 13–28.

There were tensions in these very early days of the Church. Some favored a more Jewish form of Christianity. Paul argued that this was "another gospel," and that the New Law as preached by Jesus Christ should be followed.

After much dispute with those who wanted to preserve the Christian ties with the Jewish tradition, Paul's argument won out. The Church would be built on the foundation of the New Law as taught by Christ himself.

Dissension and Persecution

Christian historians report that late in his life and ministry, the chief apostle Peter made his way to Rome, the capital city of the Roman Empire, preaching the apostolic faith and establishing a Christian community. Paul, a convert from Judaism, also traveled through the Gentile world; and he, too, after "journeying often," arrived at Rome. It was there that both Peter and Paul met their deaths, probably in the same year (64), at the orders of the emperor Nero (37–68).

This was the beginning of 300 years of persecution for the Christians by the Roman authorities. Most of the persecution was local and intermittent. Occasionally, it extended to a general persecution of all the Christians in the empire. Such a persecution occurred under the emperor Decius (201–251), in 250. Decius demanded that all citizens of the empire sacrifice to the Roman gods. Those Christians who refused to do so were

■ *Saints Peter and Paul* by Masolino da Panicale (1383– c. 1447). Peter carries "the keys to the kingdom of heaven" promised him by Christ (Matt. 16.19). Paul holds a two-edged sword, mentioned in Epistle to the Hebrew (4.2): "The word of God is living and effective, sharper than a two-edged sword…."

imprisoned, tortured, or killed. Many Christians died for their faith. Their martyrdom sowed the seeds of faith in the hearts of many converts. For those persecuted after the manner of Christ, it turned an era of suffering and bloodshed into an age of promise for a harvest of new believers.

As Christianity grew, its troubles and growing pains came not only from the external source of the Roman authorities, but also from its own ranks, when Christians struggled to interpret the meaning of the Gospel and its essential contents. From the beginning, Christianity was not limited to the performance of certain rituals, nor even to a certain code of moral behavior, but proclaimed a new message that touched upon the whole of reality in all of its depth and breadth. The proper interpretation of this message of the Gospel was sometimes the subject of disagreement and debate. At various points in its history, the Christian community has had to declare which interpretations were consistent with the essential message of the Gospel and which were not. Those that were not were called heresies, meaning that they were misinterpretations of the message of the Gospel. The interpretations that were consistent with the essential message of the Gospel were declared "correct" or "orthodox." The writers of the early Christian Church who explained and defended the orthodox teaching were later called "the Fathers of the Church." They earned this title because they were considered to be the begetters of spiritual children who held to the true faith. The earliest were Ignatius of Antioch (30–107), Clement of Rome (30–100), Justin Martyr (c.100–c.165), and Irenaeus (120–202). They were later joined by Clement of Alexandria (c.150–c.215), Origen (c.185–254), Tertullian (c.155–c.220), and Cyprian (200–258).

The Gradual Acceptance of Christianity

After many years of rejection and persecution, Christians began to gain some acceptance. At first, they were merely tolerated. However, by the time of Constantine (280–337), who is considered the first Christian emperor of Rome, they had achieved favored status. Around 380, Christianity became the accepted religion of Rome.

■ *The fish became a symbol of Christ for early Christians, since the Greek word for fish was* **icthus**, *which was an abbreviation for* **Iesus Christos theou uios soter** *(Jesus Christ, the Son of God, Savior).*

Tensions between Eastern and Western Christianity

Not only had Constantine made Christianity the favored religion of the empire, he had also moved the empire's capital in 330 from Rome to Byzantium, which he renamed Constantinople. This seat of political power became then a center of ecclesiastical importance. Rome retained a primacy of honor, but Constantinople, Antioch, Alexandria, and Jerusalem in the Eastern half of the Roman Empire were regional centers that made claims of independence in the running of the regional churches under their care.

On important matters of belief, the regional and local bishops or their representatives from Rome, Constantinople, Antioch, Alexandria, and Jerusalem, along with their doctrinal advisers, gathered together in general, or ecumenical, councils. The first such council was held at Nicea (325), where Arius, who denied the divinity of Christ, was condemned as a heretic. The second ecumenical council, held at Constantinople (381), formulated a creed, or statement, of fundamental Christian beliefs, recited in Catholic and Eastern Orthodox Churches today, called the Constantinopolitan/Nicene Creed.

■ *Later Fathers of the Church who fought Arianism, Nestorianism, Monophysitism, and other heresies:*

Ambrose of Milan (c.339–397)

Athanasius (c.293–373)

Augustine of Hippo (c.354–430)

Basil of Caesarea (c.330–379)

Cyril of Alexandria (c.375–444)

Cyril of Jerusalem (c.315–387)

Eusebius of Caesarea (c.260–339)

Gregory of Nazianzen (c.330–389)

Gregory of Nyssa (c.330–395)

Hilary of Poitiers (c.315–367)

John Chrysostom (c.344–407)

The first doctrinal breaks in the unity of the Christian Church occurred in the 5th century. The Council of Ephesus (431) condemned Nestorius for teaching that there were two persons in Christ, and the Council of Chalcedon (451) condemned the Monophysites who taught that there was only one nature, a divine nature, in Christ. The "nestorian" Church in Iran, known today as the Assyrian Church of the East, separated from the orthodox, or correct, teaching followed by Rome and the remaining Eastern Churches after the Council of Ephesus. The "monophysite" Churches of Armenia, Syria, Egypt, Ethiopia, and India, known today as the "Oriental Orthodox Churches", broke away from the orthodox Churches after the Council of Chalcedon. The Eastern Churches that affirmed the orthodox teachings became known as the "Eastern Orthodox" Churches.

The History of the Western Church

Early Problems in the Western Church

The Roman acceptance of Christianity gradually brought with it a number of problems. One internal problem was that

■ *Benedictine monks, men of work and prayer, followed the plan of life of St. Benedict. One of the most famous places where they lived was Monte Cassino, located almost a hundred miles south of Rome. Here is a sketch of three monks found in the library of Monte Cassino, Italy. Its title reads, "Chapter VI: Concerning Monks."*

whereas in the past being a Christian often came at personal risk, now it was conventional and even socially advantageous to be a Christian. Thus, there was an increasing number of Christians who were not very serious about their faith. Perhaps as a reaction to this phenomenon, some Christians began to search for ways to live out their faith in a more perfect manner.

One such way was the development of monasticism, which was a movement that began in Egypt in the 4th century and quickly spread throughout the Christian world. The monastic movement is the ancient source of the present-day religious orders in the Roman Catholic Church and the communities of monks and nuns in the Eastern Orthodox and Eastern Catholic Churches. The origins of the monastic movement are usually traced back to a man named Anthony (251–356), who lived in Egypt in the 4th century. Monastic life entailed a withdrawal from worldly affairs in favor of dedication to a religious life of poverty, chastity, and obedience.

Another problem raised by Christianity's acceptance by the Roman world was that many non-Christians began to blame Christianity for the declining fortunes of the Roman Empire. Rome in its glory days, when pagan gods and the emperors were worshiped, was militarily strong. As Christianity gained a foothold, Rome found itself under the threat of extinction by invaders from the North. Some Roman citizens began to raise serious questions about the role of Christians and Christianity in the empire. Would Christians be good citizens who could be depended on to fight for Rome? Or were they so committed to Christ's kingdom that earthly kingdoms and responsibilities had no importance for them? In short, where did the Christians put their loyalty? To which kingdom did they belong—the heavenly one or the earthly one? As the debate went on, Rome fell.

The Early Roman Papacy

After the fall of Rome, the Catholic Church in the West could quite well have fallen into a collection of small feudal churches controlled by local lords. If there was a uniting force that prevented this ecclesiastical splintering, it was the Roman papacy. The primacy of honor for Rome had been admitted by the Eastern patriarchates, but it never grew into a primacy of jurisdiction. Nor was the political ruler of the Roman Empire in Constantinople willing to admit a higher human force to which

◼ Pope Gregory I, or Gregory the Great, was the first monk to become a pope. Here he dictates to his scribe a sermon inspired by the Holy Spirit, who, in the form of a dove, sits on his right shoulder.

he must submit. The model of the Roman Empire was based on a regal-sacerdotal view of government: religious concerns were subordinate to imperial interests.

Pope Gregory I, or Gregory the Great, who ruled from 590 to 604, was the first monk to become pope. Gregory, however, was not a monk totally cut off from the world. He was politically sophisticated. He had been papal representative to the imperial court at Constantinople for a number of years before his election to the papacy. His reign was outstanding. In circumstances that were very trying, he fed the poor of Rome. He managed the estates of the Church in such a way that the crops were consistently abundant, and the workers were treated with great humanity. He reformed church music and the celebration of worship within the Church, and he preached fervently and frequently. His greatest achievement, perhaps, was his effort to bring Christianity and its message to a bigger world. He realized that popes or their legates in the Eastern Empire were the subjects of the emperor. In their civil capacity they were, thus, under the ruler's jurisdiction. How could a true Christian society be built, one in which a Christian view of human fulfillment could be fostered? Gregory, who saw his papal office as a responsibility to bring about the Christianization of all men, set his hopes on the Western Empire.

In his initial effort to accomplish his mission, Gregory sent Augustine of Canterbury (d.604) as the head of a small group of missionaries to bring the Christian life and faith to England. A number of Gregory's contemporaries also carried Christianity to other parts of Europe. For example, Columban (c.521–597), an Irish monk, preached to the Franks. A century later, Boniface (c.675–754) converted the Germanic peoples. In the latter part of the 10th century, Christianity made rapid headway in Denmark, Sweden, and Norway. The call to baptize all nations was being accomplished.

The Flourishing of Religious Life

Monastic life began to flourish, and it breathed new spiritual life into the Christianity of Rome, which then spread throughout the Western world. Benedict of Nursia (c.480–c.547) founded a number of monasteries, first at Subiaco, in the mountain region east of Rome, and then in a dozen other locations. These were independent, self-supporting, and self-contained communities of monks, just outside towns or in rural areas. They were dedicated to prayer, work, and study. The monastic life demands that persons withdraw from worldly affairs to devote themselves completely to religion.

The houses where monks or nuns live are called abbeys, and they are ruled over by abbots (spiritual fathers). The life of devotion in these abbeys was organized around the Divine Office. This office consisted of the Book of Psalms, readings from the Old and New Testaments, readings from the early church fathers, and hymns. This book of prayer was structured so that all 150 psalms of the Old Testament were sung each week, with each day divided into eight parts. Every three hours, a part of this Divine Office was chanted.

This schedule brought to the whole day a spirit of prayer, so that even work and study were done within a prayerful atmosphere. Benedict's Rule was sturdy enough on its own, and without any common government it was able to keep order within the many independent monasteries as they multiplied. At times, these monasteries became too strongly supported by the wealthy and politically powerful. Often the result was a relaxation of monastic discipline. When this happened, reforms often took place, as they did at Citeaux and Cluny in France in the late 11th and early 12th centuries.

Other religious movements gained prominence, especially in the 12th and 13th centuries. As cities began to sprout up throughout Europe, a new kind of ministry was needed besides the one carried on in the monasteries, which were usually separated from urban life. Two of the most influential movements were begun by Saint Francis of Assisi (1181–1226) and by Saint Dominic (1170–1221). They founded two religious orders, the Franciscans and the Dominicans, dedicated to poverty and preaching. The Franciscans and Dominicans also founded female communities: the Poor Claires, followers of Claire of Assisi, and Dominican Sisters. They also established lay associates, called Third Order Franciscans or Third Order Dominicans.

Lean le Clerc excu

■ *Saint Francis of Assisi is one of the most popular saints in Christian history. He is known for his pursuit of a life of poverty, his love of nature, and his imitation of Christ. The stigmata is the sign of his life devoted to following the crucified Christ.*

The Prayer of Saint Francis of Assisi

Lord, make me an instrument of your peace.
Where there is hatred, let me sow love;
Where there is injury, pardon;
Where there is doubt, faith;
Where there is despair, hope;
Where there is darkness, light;
And where there is sadness, joy.
O Divine Master,
grant that I may not so much seek to be consoled as to console;
to be understood as to understand;
to be loved as to love.
For it is in giving that we receive;
it is in pardoning that we are pardoned,
and it is in dying that we are born to eternal life.

The Christian Teaching Mission

In the same year, 529, that Rome fell to invaders, the Benedictine monastery of Monte Cassino was founded. It was in this monastery that many of the literary and scientific works of the Roman world were copied and preserved for the future. The writings of Cicero (106–43 B.C.E.), Virgil (70–19 B.C.E.), and Seneca (4 B.C.E.–65 C.E.), and the many other educators of Rome, were copied by the monastic scribes. These works, along with the Bible, formed the building blocks of the educational reform of Charlemagne (742–814) that was headed by the Irish monk Alcuin (735–804). Eventually schools developed that were linked to monasteries as well as to palaces and cathedrals. Monks and priests, civil clerks, and administrators were educated at these schools. Later, from some of these schools emerged the first universities located in Bologna, Paris, and Oxford.

When the universities began, the Franciscans and Dominicans also became strong participants in the intellectual life there. Among the most famous thinkers of the Middle Ages were Albert the Great (c.1200–1280) and Thomas Aquinas (1224–1274), both Dominicans, and Bonaventure (c.1217–1274), Duns Scotus (1266–1308), and William of Ockham (c.1285–c.1347), who were Franciscans. These religious orders also produced well-respected preachers such as Raymond of Penafort (1185–1275), Anthony of Padua (1195–1231), Bernardine of Siena (1380–1444), and John Capistran (1385–1456).

The Medieval Papacy at its Height

Over the centuries, slow step by slow step, the papacy gained its independence from Constantinople. Pepin, the King of the Franks from 751–768, helped the papacy to obtain independent territories in central Italy by fighting the Lombards who were threatening Rome. When Pope Leo III (795–815) conferred the imperial crown on Pepin's son, Charlemagne (800–814), thereby declaring him emperor of the Romans, he made the Church independent of Constantinople and the Eastern Empire. Gregory VII (1073–1085) established a system of Church laws and revised papal administration, so that the papacy entered upon the path of effective rulership by means of law. The life of a Christian on earth, a life according to church law, determined his life in the other world. Supporting itself by the Bible, patristic teachings, and earlier papal doctrine, the papacy established itself as the divinely instituted government of the Western Christian world. The Church was the congregation of the faithful entrusted by Christ to the pope, through Saint Peter and his successors. Its goal was otherworldly, and none other than the holder of the keys of the kingdom of heaven knew by virtue of his office how to achieve this highest end.

Gregory the Great had set a wonderful example for the papacy, and it was followed by many splendid instances of strong and religious popes in the 11th century: Leo IX (1048–1054), Alexander II (1061–1073), and Gregory VII (1073–1085) are but a few. These reformers tried to keep the spiritual power of the papacy free from the control of government rulers and to separate the appointment of bishops from government powers. The 12th century also revealed many strong popes: Innocent II (1130–1143), Eugene III (1145–1153), Alexander II (1159–1181), and Innocent III (1198–1216). They too opposed the dominance of the government rulers of their times and their invasion into the realm of religious authority. There also were at times popes who did not follow Gregory's example. They were weak, or conniving, or sinful in other ways. Yet, a basic distinction between the office and the person remained dominant in the world of the medieval papacy. The medieval world did not consider any formula for separating the temporal from the spiritual, so both good and bad persons could hold good offices. It was the office of the pope, or bishop, or teacher that commanded respect even when the person holding it might distract from its dignity.

The Crusades

The crusades were a series of attempts from the 11th to the 15th centuries under the direction of the popes to free the Holy Land from the Turks. Initiated by Urban II (1088–1099) in 1095, the crusades were portrayed as a pilgrimage and were crowned with an indulgence equal to a lifetime of penance: "If any man sets out to free the Church of God at Jerusalem out of pure devotion and not out of love for glory or gain, the journey shall be accounted a complete penance on his part." In 1099, Jerusalem was taken and the Muslim population was killed or conquered. Throughout the succeeding crusades, however, dissension among the leaders took place and deviations from their holy purpose often led to failure. The assaults on the Muslims, and on the Greeks through whose lands they travelled during these attempts to rescue the Holy Land, have left deep-rooted hatreds even to the present.

Inquisitions

Inquisitions were also instituted by popes. Pope Gregory IX (1227–1241) established the Medieval Inquisition in 1229 to bring legal procedures to the condemnations of Albigensian heretics. The Albigensians, similar to the Manicheans, admitted two principles as the source of the universe: a good principle that created spiritual reality and a bad principle that created material things. Their way of life and dress was simple, and they attacked the worldliness of the clergy. They also rejected the Old Testament and opposed infant baptism, since it lacked a personal commitment to Christ. Condemned at the Council of Albi in 1176, they continued to survive. Pope Gregory attempted to establish legal means for dealing with these heretics to put an end to the wars that were erupting against them. A few hundred years later, in 1478, a different form of inquisition was founded by Ferdinand (1452–1516) and Isabella (1479–1504) in Spain. The Spanish Inquisition was a more pronouncedly civil instrument that attempted to promote religion as a means of achieving political unity and to condemn those who were suspected of false political affiliation as threats to Christian life and ideals. In all, the medieval period shows, in its popes, its crusades, and in its inquisitions, the great influence of the papacy and its frequent battles against and seductions by worldly powers.

Divisions Among the Christian Churches of the West

Splits from the Catholic Church, reminiscent of those at Ephesus (431) and Chalcedon (451), also took place in the West. Differing opinions and views once again caused problems among Christians. Does God save man without man's efforts? Or does man merit heaven by his own good works? Is the Bible alone a sufficient guide for a Christian, or is the Catholic Church the divinely appointed authority for interpreting its message?

Martin Luther (1483–1546), an Augustinian monk, raised such issues in the 95 theses he nailed to the door of Wittenberg

Cathedral in Germany on October 31, 1517. He accused the Roman Catholic Church of being too involved with political and material ambition. In his pamphlet "On Christian Liberty," he established the division between the political and spiritual, the natural and the supernatural, the human and the divine. According to Luther, the Roman Church had compromised too much with this world. It had blurred the distinction between political and religious power with its theory of merit by human efforts and by its doctrine on indulgences, whereby people could claim heavenly rewards in exchange for money.

The religious world, according to Luther, should be more spiritual and less worldly. Luther's basic premise, was that religion should always be criticizing those who are attached to worldly things and earthly power. Many other efforts at reform, frequently with separating tendencies, followed Luther's lead. Ulrich Zwingli (1484–1531), Guillaume Farel (1489–1565), Martin Bucer (1491–1551), and John Calvin (1509–1564) all preached reform and eventually separated from the Roman Church. Even Roman Catholicism itself began to see reform.

Catholic Reformation

The Catholic Church throughout its history often sought reform for its infidelities to the Gospel teachings. This is evident from the reforms of Benedictine life in the 11th and 12th centuries at Citeau and Cluny in France. Bernard of Clairvaux (1090–1153), less than 20 years after the founding of the Cistercian Order at Citeau in 1098, was pushing for even further reforms of Citeau. For Bernard, the monks had too many associations with rich supporters. He attacked the ornateness of their cloisters: "If the monks are engrossed in their reading [of the Scriptures], what is the purpose of these ludicrous monstrosities, this incredibly distorted beauty and perfection of ugliness?" He felt that monasteries need not mimick castles.

The need for church reform on a broader level was also clear from the church laws which were developed throughout the Middle Ages to guide and direct the life and activities of the Church. In Italy during the 14th century, Girolamo Savonarola (1452–1498) preached against church abuses, as did Francisco

Ximenes (1436–1517) in Spain. Pope Adrian VI (1522–1523) admitted that corruption had touched even the highest levels of the prelates and clergy. In 1542, Pope Paul III (1534–1549) called for a General Council of the Church at Trent to express more clearly the teachings of the Church and to institute reform in the religious life of its members. This council attempted to state the differences between Catholic and Protestant teachings. It also established seminaries or schools for the training of priests in correct Catholic teaching and exemplary living. During his pon-

■ *Hermanos Zuccarelli's 1560's portrayal of the pope, bishops, and theologians at the Council of Trent.*

tificate, Paul III also gave formal approval to the Society of Jesus, the Jesuit order founded by Ignatius of Loyola (1491–1556) in 1534. The Jesuits played a leading role in education and in the Church's program of spiritual renewal.

Challenges to Catholicism from the 17th to the 19th Centuries

Despite the strong and successful efforts of the Church to renew Christian life among its members in the years after the Council of Trent, ever new challenges to the Church kept arising.

Due to the conflicts between Catholic and Protestant citizens in the countries of Europe, all Christian religions now began to be questioned. Toleration of religious differences was appealed to by the philosopher John Locke (1632–1704) in his essay *On Toleration*, written during his exile from England in the 1680s.

The basic assumptions of Locke's work are that the teachings of any church are opinions which men hold, and every reasonable opinion should be respected. Men simply choose to join a religion the way they choose to belong to any organization. Religious gatherings and celebrations are permitted on the same terms as a dinner meeting of an extended family or a club. In short, religious rituals are treated in the same way as a secular event: a Eucharistic liturgy is simply an act of eating bread and wine. Catholics claim that during the Mass the bread and wine become the body and blood of Christ. Locke would claim that Catholics have a right to believe such a thing as long as it does not harm anyone. Yet, at the same time he would argue that such a belief is not true—a position unacceptable to the Catholic Church.

Other writers, such as Jean-Jacques Rousseau (1712–1778) in *The Social Contract* of 1762, likewise promoted the religion of what came to be called the Age of Reason. Rousseau argued for a secular religion that would alone be beneficial to society and would avoid the conflicts often engendered by Catholic or Protestant faiths. His religion would have just a few tenets that all men of goodwill would surely accept: there is a God who exists, and he is all-knowing. Men have souls that survive death. God rewards the good and punishes the wicked, including those who do not live up to the obligations of their contracts.

Other forces within society also raised challenges against the Church. The desire on the part of kings, especially in France, to control the appointment of bishops, brought great tensions between popes and kings. Kings started to appoint the bishops in the territories they controlled and thus undermined papal influence. Under such conditions, the Church in particular countries became a puppet of the king. As democracy and revolution attacked the king, they also began to attack the Church, whose hierarchy had been appointed by the king.

The Catholic Response

The leadership of the Church was strengthened under two long-reigning popes in the second half of the 19th century. Pope Pius IX (1846–1878), who convened the First Vatican Council (1869–1870), re-established respect for the papacy. The council itself, through its declaration of the infallibility of the pope, also strengthened the teaching authority of the papacy and ensured its independence in the spiritual realm from the control of secular rulers.

Pius's successor, Leo XIII (1878–1903), made strong efforts to convince liberal secular leaders that they and the Church could live in harmony. He tried to deal with the modern world on many levels. In education, he proclaimed Thomas Aquinas as a solid example of Catholic thinking that could deal well with the challenges presented by modern philosophers like Locke and Rousseau. On another level, Leo XIII kept close contact with everyday problems of ordinary Catholics and addressed them through letters. These encyclical letters, or letters addressed to the universal church, often dealt with social issues that touched the daily lives of Catholic working people. Through his stimulation, Roman Catholicism became even more socially active.

The Modern Catholic Response to Social Issues

At the end of the 19th and the beginning of the 20th centuries, responding to the needs of the large number of poor immigrants who needed assistance in getting food, housing, and work in their new homeland of America, the Church that seemed to be losing influence in a number of secular societies in Europe began gaining in numbers and dedication in lands outside of Europe. With the wave of immigrants from Ireland, Italy, southern Germany, Poland, Portugal, and Spain, for example, Roman Catholicism began to have strong influence once again, this time in North America.

The Catholic Church took its most dramatic step in its effort to relate to modern secular culture and other religions at the Second Vatican Council. This council which lasted from 1962 to 1965 was initiated by Pope John XXIII (1958–1963) and was completed by Pope Paul VI (1963–1978). Its important document, the

Constitution on the Church, gave ordinary people a greater active role in church life and granted bishops a greater share in the authority of the Church. Pope John Paul II, who grew up under Communist rule in Poland, has continued to promote a more active involvement of the Catholic Church in society. He has made frequent visits to his flock throughout the world and in particular has addressed young Catholics whom he views as the flourishing future of the Church.

The History of the Eastern Churches

Split from Rome

Tensions between the Eastern Churches and Rome arose shortly after the Roman Empire was separated into Eastern and Western halves at the end of the 3rd century. Each part of the empire eventually had its own emperor and language. The East spoke Greek, and the West spoke Latin. These political and linguistic differences have made attempts at union difficult throughout history and the split still remains.

The first real, though partial, split came with the Nestorian and Monophysite heresies condemned at the Councils of Ephesus (431) and Chalcedon (451). A much more serious separation occurred in 1054, when all the Eastern Churches became separated from the Roman Catholic Church and became known as the "Eastern Orthodox Churches." The two main issues involved in this separation were the primacy of the pope and the manner of explaining the doctrine of the Trinity. The Eastern Orthodox accepted the pope as the most honored bishop of the Christian world, but he was still one bishop among many. They thus did not believe that the pope should have direct authority over all Christians. They also refused to accept the Roman Catholic teaching concerning the relationship of the Holy Spirit to the Father and the Son. For the Eastern Churches, the Holy Spirit proceeds from the Father alone. The Roman Catholic Church declares that the Holy Spirit proceeds from the Father and the Son. The disagreements became so intense that they led to the mutual excommunication of the patriarch of Constantinople and the papal legate. The lengthy process of

■ The domes of Trinity
Monastery, founded by
Saint Sergius in 1345.
This monastery has
been the center of
Russian Orthodoxy
for hundreds of years.

estrangement continued until it culminated in a complete split upon the sack of Constantinople by the Latin Crusaders in 1204.

Increasingly, the main center of Eastern Christianity shifted northward to the Slavic countries. The conversion of the Slavs to Eastern Christianity began in the 9th century, through the missionary work of two Greek brothers, Cyril (c.827–869) and Methodius (c.825–885). As a result of their efforts, Eastern Christianity spread to Bulgaria, Serbia, and Russia. Cyril and Methodius are thus recognized in the Eastern tradition as "apostles of the Slavs." Eastern Christianity became the official state religion of Russia in 988 with the conversion of Prince Vladimir (956–1015). Vladimir was a devoted Christian who tried to rule his country in a Christian manner, initiating the ideal of a "holy Russia." Monasteries and Christian culture thrived under his rule. The tradition of icon painting flourished during that time. One of the most famous religious images of Christendom, the icon of the Holy Trinity, by Saint Andrei Rublev (c.1360–1430), dates from this period of Russian culture.

Eastern Christianity in the Middle Ages

Separated from the West, Eastern Christianity continued to develop its own distinctive approach to Christian life. An important development of Eastern Christianity in the Middle Ages was the movement of "quietness." This practice began with Eastern monks who engaged in continual efforts at placing themselves in the presence of Jesus. Often they would do this by praying the "Jesus prayer": "Lord Jesus Christ, Son of the living God, have mercy on me, a sinner." Many of these monks claimed that they had attained a certain union with God through these exercises, purging themselves of other concerns. Others criticized them, insisting that God could not be directly experienced. One of the great figures of the Eastern Christian tradition, Saint Gregory Palamas (1296–1359), resolved the issue by explaining that although men cannot participate in God's being, people can experience God's energies, or grace, operating in them. Eastern Christians to this day place a great value on meditating on the Jesus prayer. They often use a prayer rope, which looks much like a rosary, to assist them in this practice.

From the early centuries of Christianity to the 15th century, the center of Eastern Christianity was Constantinople, the capital of the Byzantine or Eastern Roman Empire. But in 1453, Constantinople was sacked by the Turks. The Greek Constantinople became Istanbul. Eastern Christians continued to live and practice their faith under the Turkish rule of the Ottoman Empire, but they were made to pay special taxes and the spread of their faith was curtailed, since any form of missionary activity was forbidden.

The Eastern Catholic Churches

Eastern Catholic Churches came into existence when groups of Orthodox Christians sought reunion with the Church of Rome after the division between East and West in 1054. Eastern Catholics have the same religious practices as the Eastern Orthodox, and they share the same history as their counterparts in the Orthodox Churches up to the point when they established their reunion with Rome.

The following is a list of some major Eastern Catholic Churches and the date of their reunion with the Church of Rome.

- Ukrainian Catholic Church: 1595
- Ruthenian Catholic Church: 1646
- Syrian Catholic Church: 1656
- Melkite Catholic Church: 1724
- Armenian Catholic Church: 1742
- Chaldean Catholic Church (present-day Iraq): 1834
- Coptic (Egyptian) Catholic Church: 1899

All of the above Catholic Churches have Orthodox counterparts. Other Eastern Catholic Churches include the Syro-Malabar Catholic Church and the Syro-Malankara Catholic Church, both in India; the Romanian Catholic Church, the Bulgarian Catholic Church, the Slovak Catholic Church, and the Hungarian Catholic Church. Some Eastern Catholic Churches do not have an Orthodox counterpart and have always maintained communion with Rome. Such is the case with the Maronite Catholic Church, which is the major Christian Church of Lebanon.

Eastern Catholic Population Statistics:	
The Coptic Catholic Church	197,878
The Ethiopian Catholic Church	201,549
The Syro-Malankara Catholic Church	446,220
The Maronite Catholic Church	3,124,086
The Syrian Catholic Church	137,166
The Armenian Catholic Church	362,047
The Albanian Catholic Church	2,474
The Bulgarian Catholic Church	15,000
Eparchy of Krizevci	148,775
The Greek Catholic Church	2,340
The Hungarian Catholic Church	278,000
The Italo-Albanian Catholic Church	61,563
The Melkite Greek Catholic Church	1,251,300
The Romanian Greek Catholic Church	1,390,610
The Ruthenian Catholic Church	662,820
The Slovak Catholic Church	221,044
The Ukrainian Greek Catholic Church	5,159,633
The Chaldean Catholic Church	322,266
The Syro-Malabar Catholic Church	3,400,093

At the Second Vatican Council, a general council of the Catholic Church held at Vatican City from 1962–1965, in the *Decree on Eastern Catholic Churches* and the *Decree on the Ministry and Life of Priests,* the council reasserted the equality of Eastern Catholic Churches with the Latin Rite; and while stressing that an unmarried way of life was a necessary requirement for Latin Rite priests, it did not change the discipline that allowed married priests in the Eastern Rite Catholic Churches.

Modern Challenges to the Eastern Orthodox Churches

Different challenges have been presented to the various Eastern Orthodox Churches in the 20th century. The Russian revolution of 1917 and the rise of the Communist party caused great suffering and confusion in Russia. It also caused a split among the Russian Orthodox Christians. In 1920, some Orthodox Russians who were in exile from their homeland instituted an independent church which came to be known as "The Russian Orthodox Church Outside Russia." They elected their own bishop in defiance of the Soviet appointees. The Russian Orthodox Church based in Moscow has repeatedly appealed for reunion with these schismatic Churches, but the restoration of unity has not yet occurred. Other Orthodox Churches have suffered similar divisions based on different views. For example questions such as whether the Orthodox Churches should engage in dialogue with other Christian Churches (ecumenism) or whether they should base their liturgical year on the old "Julian" calendar, named after Julius Caesar (100–44 B.C.E.) and authoritative for Eastern countries, or on the new "Gregorian" calendar, named after Pope Gregory XIII (1572–1585) that has been adopted over the years by most modern civil governments.

Other problems beset many of the Orthodox Churches in America. Political and cultural oppositions between home countries gradually seemed artificial to church members in the United States. Movements were formed to rise above ethnic differences. Even new churches were formed that attempted to make their communities more American or more ecumenical. Such an attempt is the Orthodox Church of America whose membership has now reached over one million faithful.

Eastern Orthodox Churches after the Breakup of the Soviet Union

When the Iron Curtain came down in Eastern Europe, many of the Orthodox Churches received new life. Many Eastern monasteries, churches, and parishes began to recover their lands, their communities of worshipers, and their vitality. Overcoming the seventy-five years of suppression will take time, but for many of these churches a second spring has arrived.

In the United States, many Orthodox Christians are now engaged in the effort to unite all American Orthodox Christians into one church that transcends ethnic boundaries and seeks to

communicate the rich traditions of Orthodoxy in the common language of American culture.

Still, particular Orthodox Churches in America continue to flourish. A good example is the Greek Orthodox Church. It has founded its own college, Hellenic College, in Boston, and despite strong competition from non-Greek schools, it has continued to draw a consistent student body. Its seminary has a respected faculty that is part of the theological cooperative called The Boston Theological Consortium.

Pope John Paul II's Attempts at Unity with Orthodox Christians

Pope John Paul II has made deliberate attempts at establishing a dialogue between Roman Catholic and Orthodox Christians in recent years. This effort has been punctuated by his stops in Greece and other countries as he retraced the steps of the Apostle Paul on his 2001 visit to the Holy Land. It is evident also in his more recent visit to Romania and his planned trip to Russia. These attempts at reconciliation with the Eastern Christian world are undertaken with hope, and also with a realistic sense of the historic events that have kept these Churches separated for nearly a thousand years. The task of seeking union is very challenging. The visit to Romania raised fears in that country and in Russia that the pope was meddling in internal Orthodox affairs, supporting an independent Romanian Orthodox Church that wants to separate from the influence of the Moscow patriarchate. Others interpreted it as part of a push by Rome to get back property that belonged to the Romanian Catholic Church. The property had been confiscated by the Russians under the reign of Joseph Stalin and given to the Romanian Orthodox Church that was united with the Moscow patriarchate. Many others saw it as an honest gesture on the part of the pope to promote the unity of the churches. A knowledge of the history of the relations between the Eastern and Western Churches and a knowledge of their structures and traditions helps to put into perspective the challenging complexities that any attempts at unity must face.

CHAPTER **4**

Catholicism and Orthodox Christianity: Their Basic Beliefs and Practices

*B*oth the Catholic and Eastern Orthodox Churches place a great value on doctrine, a set of beliefs that describes the community's experience of God's revelation and salvation. They hold that these beliefs are ultimately derived from the Bible, as it has been interpreted through church councils, the teachings of the ancient Fathers of the Church, and short statements of belief called creeds (such as the Apostle's Creed and the Nicene Creed). For Catholics and Orthodox Christians, tradition provides the authoritative interpretation of scripture.

For these churches, the two central doctrines, or beliefs, of Christianity are these truths which are affirmed in all the creeds accepted by the Catholic and Orthodox Churches:

- the belief that although there is only one God, there are three persons (Father, Son, and Holy Spirit) in God
- the belief that the Son of God became human

God thus was incarnated, meaning that he took on human flesh or became human in the person of Jesus Christ. The first belief, the belief in the Holy Trinity, was revealed by Christ, who spoke of his Father and promised the apostles that he would send

the Holy Spirit. In his life and teachings, in the miracles that he worked, and in his resurrection from the dead, Jesus Christ was revealed to his disciples as divine. Jesus thus taught his disciples to experience God as threefold, as Father, Son, and Holy Spirit. They prayed to each as God, because they recognized that the three are perfectly united in being and are one God.

The Doctrine of the Trinity

Both Roman Catholics and Eastern Orthodox Christians adhere to this doctrine of God. The Eastern liturgy suggests how God as three persons can be experienced to some small degree by thinking about love: "Let us love one another in order that we may confess the Father, the Son, and the Holy Spirit, Trinity, one in being, and undivided." If we love someone we are united with them in a special way. Since God is perfect, then his love will also be perfect. The union among the persons in God will thus be so perfect that they will be united as one.

The Doctrine of Sin

For Catholics and Eastern Orthodox Christians, humanity was created for the purpose of sharing in God's own life. They believe that God ordained this purpose for humanity when he created people according to his own image and likeness, as is told in Genesis, the first book of the Bible. However, for Catholics and Orthodox Christians, the sin of disobedience to God's command by the first man, Adam, interfered with God's plan. By disobeying God, human beings lost their way and became inclined to further disobedience and sin. Catholics speak of this condition as "original sin," which means that everyone is born into the world with some inclination toward sin.

While the Christian Bible recounts the story of human sinfulness throughout history, it depicts God's primary response to human sinfulness as one of mercy. Catholics and Orthodox Christians believe that the greatest act of God's mercy occurred when God sent his own Son into our human condition. They believe that God the Son became human, not by losing his divinity, but by combining his divinity with our humanity. Jesus Christ is one person who contains both divine and human natures. This combination healed humanity and transformed it into a humanity that is empowered by divine life. By dying on the cross, Christ killed the power of death and destroyed the root of evil. By his resurrection, he showed the victory of God over death and evil and the new life that is now open to all those who believe in him. Catholics and Orthodox Christians believe that this new life can be shared by all his followers through faith and through participation in the sacraments of the Church. This is a process that begins on earth. It is only completed after death. Thus, they say in their creed (statement of beliefs): "We believe in the Resurrection of the dead and the life of the world to come."

One difference between Catholics and Orthodox Christians is the concept of "purgatory," which is present in Roman Catholic doctrine but not in Eastern Christianity. According to Roman Catholic doctrine, when the soul leaves the body in death, it goes to one of three places: heaven, purgatory, or hell. Heaven is the community of those who made amends for their forgiven sins and who have been united with God. Purgatory is a temporary state for those who must be purified of imperfection or make amends for sins already forgiven. Hell is the endless absence of God, the punishment for persons who have rejected God through the enormity of their unrepented sins.

The Importance of Saints

Roman Catholics and Eastern Christians place a great value on the honoring of saints. To Catholics, saints are persons who have led exceptionally holy lives and who have been formally recognized by the Church as having achieved an honored position in heaven and as being entitled to devotion on earth. For many Catholics and Orthodox Christians, the saints are examples to imitate and from whom to draw inspiration. Statues of the saints are often prominently displayed in Roman Catholic churches, as are icons (religious images) of saints in Eastern Orthodox and Eastern Catholic churches.

In the Latin and Eastern traditions, the greatest of the saints is considered to be Mary, the mother of Jesus. Because they believe that Jesus Christ is God, Mary is referred to as the

*■ In this icon Christ is
infolded within his
mother Mary. This icon
reflects the verse. "The
Lord whom the heavens
could not contain is con-
tained in the Virgin."*

"Mother of God." Since Christ did not have a human father but "by the power of the Holy Spirit was born of Mary," Mary is also referred to as the Blessed Virgin. The special nature of her motherhood is told in the Gospel of Luke (1.26–38), where the angel Gabriel tells Mary that she will conceive the Son of God by the power of the Holy Spirit. The faith of the Catholic and Orthodox Churches finds great significance in Mary's role as the mother of Jesus. According to this teaching, when Mary became the mother of Jesus, she also became the mother of the Church itself that descended from him. In the Gospel of John, Jesus tells his beloved disciple, John, that he is now to consider Mary his own mother: "When Jesus saw his mother and the disciple there whom he loved standing beside her, he said to his mother, 'Woman, here is your son.' Then he said to the disciple, 'Here is your mother.' And from that hour the disciple took her into his own home." (John 19.26–27)

For Catholics and Orthodox Christians, devotion to Mary is always in the context of her special relationship to Christ. The Catholic Byzantine liturgy expresses the joyous affirmation of this special relationship by singing:

In you, Virgin, full of grace, all creation does rejoice
all the orders of angels and all of the human race
God who lives eternally
took his human flesh from thee
And he made your womb a throne
wider than the heavenly places...

Worship and Liturgy

The public acts of worship that Catholics and Orthodox Christians perform together are called the liturgy. For Catholics, the central act of the liturgy is the Eucharist, generally referred to as "Mass" in the Roman Catholic tradition and "Divine Liturgy" in the Eastern tradition. The liturgy of most of the Eastern Catholic Churches is also referred to as the "Byzantine Liturgy," because it originated in the Eastern part of the Roman empire, called "Byzantium." It is also known as the Liturgy of St. John Chrysostom, who was a saint and bishop of the early church and is thought to have composed many of the prayers of this liturgy.

Weekly attendance at Sunday liturgy and attendance on special feast days, such as Christmas, are required of all church members. These are called "holy days of obligation" in the

Roman Catholic Church. In addition, Roman Catholics carry out acts of devotion to Mary and the saints, such as novenas—devotions consisting of prayers or services held on nine consecutive days or weeks. Eastern Christians also have special services honoring Mary and her role in Christ's work of salvation. These are called "Akathist," which is a Greek word meaning "standing," referring to the fact that the congregation traditionally stands while chanting the praises of Mary. Sacramentals also play an important part in both Roman Catholic and Eastern Catholic piety. Sacramentals are holy objects or actions that the Church has set apart for use as a help toward salvation. These include the crucifix, icons, and statues. Sacramental actions include the blessing of homes, of harvests, of fishing boats, and of animals.

Icons in the Eastern Churches

In the Churches of the Eastern tradition, a great value is placed on the role of icons, representations in paint or enamel of sacred personages, such as Christ or the saints. The icons themselves are venerated and considered sacred. The Eastern Christian doctrine of icons grows out of the belief that the Incarnation of God in Jesus Christ has made it possible for all material reality to be an instrument for the revelation of God's glory. Icons are not considered to be just paintings, but are viewed as communicating the presence of the person or persons whom they represent.

Eastern Christians set aside a special Sunday for celebrating the triumph of the doctrine of icons over those who opposed it. In the year 726, the Emperor Leo III (the Isaurian, 716–741) issued an order that all images and paintings in churches be covered or destroyed. This decree divided the Eastern Christian churches into two groups:

- iconoclasts, who supported the emperor's position and favored removing the images from the churches
- monks and people in general who were already used to the place of these images in devotion

Saint John of Damascus (c.675–750), a theologian, clarified the issue by explaining that icons are not worshipped but are venerated as a means to worship God. After the second Nicene council in 787, the use of icons in churches was restored and this continues in Eastern Christian churches today.

The Church Calendar

In both the Eastern Orthodox and Catholic traditions, liturgical prayer and piety is organized with a view to the seasons of the liturgical year. Throughout history, Christianity saw a progression in the development of liturgical observances. In the early years of Christianity, many Christians assumed that the Second Coming of Christ was near and that the world would soon come to an end. Up until the 4th century, the Church formally celebrated only Sundays, Easter, and Pentecost, holy days related to the redemption of mankind. As Christians began to accept that the world had not come to an end and was unlikely to come to an end any time soon, they also accepted as a reminder of ideal Christian life on earth a calendar of feast days that had been developed informally. By the Middle Ages, each day of the year honored a saint, an event, or a religious reality, such as the Trinity.

Christian holy days often transformed traditional pagan, or pre-Christian, festivals. For example, ceremonies and symbols associated with the vernal equinox—the beginning of spring—took on new depth and meaning and came to represent Christ's Resurrection. December 25th was celebrated in ancient Rome as the feast of Sol Invictus, the unconquered sun. Kindling the Yule log, decorating houses with holly and evergreens, and adorning an evergreen tree were magical pagan acts to encourage the sun's return. For Christians, Christ is the light of the world, the spiritual Sun. Christians gave the ancient pagan feast a new meaning, and many pagan symbols were converted to express different facets of the new Christian meaning.

Special Feasts and Festivals

At present, both the Roman and Eastern Catholic Churches have liturgical calendars marked by the observance of a multitude of feasts and festivals. Nevertheless, the most important of these are still the ones that commemorate the major events in the life of Jesus Christ. In the Roman Catholic tradition, the liturgical year begins in Advent, the time of preparation for the celebration of Christmas. Not long after the celebration of Christmas, the time of Lent begins, a time of preparation for the celebration of the death and Resurrection of Christ, during Holy Week. Lent, beginning with "Ash Wednesday" and extending for a period of forty days, is considered to be a time of purification and sacrifice. It is customary to "give up" something as a sign of repentance and single-minded dedication to God. After Easter comes the celebration of Pentecost, the descent of the Holy Spirit upon the apostles. As well as the Advent, Christmas, Lent, and Easter seasons, the Roman Catholic liturgical calendar also contains a period called "ordinary time," which is often interpreted as the season for focusing on how the life of Christ can be applied to one's ordinary circumstances of living in the world today as a follower of Christ.

The same major feasts are celebrated in the Eastern Christian tradition, where the liturgical year begins on September 1. The Eastern tradition places much emphasis on preparation for the major feasts of Christmas and, especially, Easter. Some form of fasting is prescribed for the period preceding both feasts. The traditional Lenten fast includes abstaining from all meat and dairy products, as well as intensified prayer and almsgiving. The highlight of the Eastern liturgical year is Easter, the Feast of the Resurrection of Christ, in which the faithful sing repeatedly:

> *Christ is risen from the dead*
> *trampling down death by death*
> *and upon those in the tomb*
> *bestowing life.*

Another climactic moment in the celebration of the Easter Liturgy in the Eastern Catholic Church is the chanting of the Easter sermon of St. John Chrysostom, which expresses the joy of Christians at the Resurrection of Christ:

> *All of you, enter into the joy of our Lord....You rich and*
> *you poor, join hands together....You who fast and you*
> *who do not, be glad today. The table is full; feast sump-*
> *tuously. The calf is ample: let no one go forth unsatis-*
> *fied. Let us all take part in the banquet of faith. Let us*
> *all take part in the wealth of righteousness. Let no one*

lament their poverty, for the Kingdom has been revealed. Let no one grieve over sins, for forgiveness has dawned from the tomb. Let no one be afraid of death, for the death of the Savior has set us free....O Death, where is your sting? O Hades, where is your victory? Christ is risen and you are overthrown. Christ is risen and the demons have fallen. Christ is risen and the angels rejoice. Christ is risen and freedom is given to life.... To him be glory and power forever and ever. Amen.

■ Feasts of the Catholic and Eastern Orthodox Churches

Among the most important universal Church observances shared by both the Catholic and Eastern Orthodox Churches are:

Lent *(period beginning forty weekdays before Easter): an annual season of fasting and penitence in preparation for Easter*

Palm Sunday *(Sunday before Easter): commemorates Christ's triumphal entry into Jerusalem*

Holy Thursday *(Thursday before Easter): celebrates Jesus' gift of his body and blood in the Eucharist; the anniversary of the Last Supper*

Good Friday *(Friday before Easter): the commemoration of the crucifixion of Christ*

Easter Sunday: *(The Sunday after Good Friday): celebrates Jesus Christ's resurrection from the dead*

Ascension Day *(fortieth day after Easter): celebrates the ascension, or rising of Christ to heaven*

Pentecost *(seventh Sunday after Easter): commemorates the descent of the Holy Spirit on the disciples*

Assumption of Mary *(known as "Dormition of Mary" in the Eastern Churches; August 15) celebrates the day on which God assumed the body of Mary into heaven*

Immaculate Conception *(December 8): celebrates the sinlessness of Mary, the mother of Christ. [Eastern Christians also recognize the sinlessness of Mary, but do not speak of it in these terms. The birth of Mary is celebrated on this day in the Eastern Churches as the* **Conception of St. Anne***, the day on which Mary was conceived by Anne, her mother.]*

Christmas *(December 25): celebrates the birth of Christ*

Top-*Cross of the Crusades, which became known as the Jerusalem cross.*

Middle-*The Chi(X) Rho(P) cross carries in it the first letters– **Ch** and **r**–in the name of **Chr**ist.*

Bottom-*The Celtic cross includes the circle of the sun, which reminds those who look at it that Christ, who died on the cross, is the Light or Sun of the spiritual world.*

Divine Liturgy and Mass

The festive character of any holy day, as well as that of regular Sundays, is centered on the celebration of the Eucharist. In both the Latin and Eastern traditions, this celebration has two main parts, the liturgy of the word and the Eucharistic Liturgy. In the Roman Catholic tradition, the liturgy of the word consists of a petition for forgiveness of sins, hymns, prayers, biblical readings, a homily or sermon concerning the biblical readings, and a declaration of faith through the recitation of the creed. The biblical readings generally follow a pattern of presenting three related texts. One text is from the Old Testament, another from the Letters of the New Testament, and the last is from one of the four Gospels. The readings also follow a cycle, so that a broad collection of scriptural readings is heard over a number of years. Listeners at Mass thus encounter the fullness of divine revelation. The homily is not intended to be a sermon covering any subject the priest might choose at random, but is meant to be an exposition of the contents of the three texts. Most of these elements are also present in the Byzantine Divine Liturgy of Eastern Christianity, which moreover includes a procession around the church with the gospel book.

The Eucharistic Liturgy is a celebration of the Lord's Supper, also known as the Last Supper—the meal Jesus shared with his disciples the evening before his crucifixion. In many ways, the structure of the Mass follows the Passover meal or Sader that Christ shared with his disciples. Gifts of bread and wine are offered to God. The priest, acting in Jesus' name and invoking the power of the Holy Spirit, changes these gifts into Christ's body and blood. The congregation then receives, under the appearance of bread and wine, the body and blood of Christ. The Catholic and Eastern Orthodox Churches teach firmly that the Eucharist involves an actual change: its members believe in faith that the sacrament is not just a symbol of Christ's body and blood; it is the body and blood of Christ. For Catholics and Orthodox Christians, the Eucharist or Divine Liturgy is a participation in the life of Christ. They believe that the church participates in the heavenly Kingdom of God through the Divine Liturgy.

The Sacraments

Other important liturgical acts of Catholic and Orthodox Christians include the sacraments. The word *sacrament* means "seal." The sacraments seal the relationship between God and the Christian community. The seven sacraments, which are all present in both Catholic and Orthodox Churches, are ceremonial signs of God's action in people's lives. Catholics believe that the sacraments are the sources, or means, by which a person attains the condition of being in the right relationship and intimate union with God. Roman Catholics refer to this condition as the "state of grace." The seven sacraments are:

■ *An iconostasis, a screen ornamented with rows of icons, separates the nave from the altar in many Eastern churches. The conversion of the bread and wine into the body and blood of Christ is a mystery that takes place beyond this screen.*

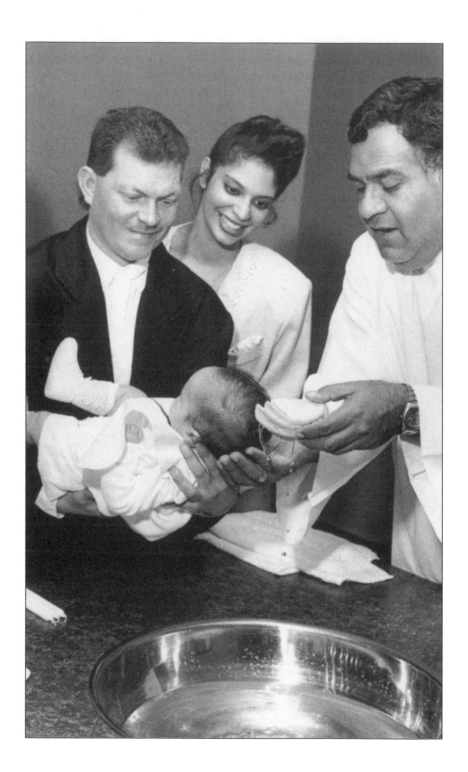

■ *A priest baptizes a young child by pouring water on the child's head, while saying, "I baptize you in the name of the Father, and of the Son, and of the Holy Spirit."*

- **Baptism:** Is the ceremony in which a child, or an adult convert, is cleansed of sin to begin a new life with God. The name of the Trinity is invoked over the person being baptized. In the Eastern Churches, the person being baptized is simultaneously immersed in water, while in the Roman Catholic Church some water is poured over the person's head. In both cases, these actions signify that the person is being cleansed of sin and that a new spiritual life is flowing into the baptized. These Christians believe that baptism also marks the beginning of a person's union with Christ and entry into the community of the Church.

- **Confirmation:** (often called "chrismation" in the Eastern tradition) Signifies the indwelling of the Holy Spirit upon the baptized person, just as the Spirit came upon the disciples on the first Pentecost. This sacrament strengthens a baptized person in the Christian faith and confers the grace that will enable that person to grow to spiritual adulthood. During this ceremony, the baptized person is marked with the sign of the cross in chrism or holy oil (a sign of strength). In the Eastern tradition, this sacrament is conferred on the baptized person immediately following the sacrament of Baptism. In the Roman Catholic tradition, the sacrament of confirmation represents the coming-of-age of the Catholic and so is not administered to infants. Another slight difference is that in the Roman Catholic Church the bishop is the ordinary minister of the sacrament of confirmation. In the Eastern Churches, a priest is also permitted to confer this sacrament on those who are to receive it.

- **The Divine Liturgy, or Mass:** Is the central act of worship for both Roman Catholics and Eastern Christians and is described above. It is the sacrament of Holy Eucharist.

- **Reconciliation:** (also called penance or confession) Is another sacrament that is shared by Catholic and Eastern Orthodox Christians. This is the sacrament of divine mercy, in which God's forgiving love is freely offered to any baptized person who seeks it, regardless of their sins. Both traditions believe that an individual's sins affect the whole church and that God's forgiveness is also offered through the church. The person who seeks God's forgiveness in this sacrament confesses his or her sins to a priest and expresses a sincere sorrow for having sinned and a willingness to refrain from future sin. In the Roman Catholic Church, the priest, as a representative of Christ, forgives the sinner with the statement: "I absolve you from your sins in the name of the Father and of the Son and of the Holy Spirit." In the Eastern tradition, the priest absolves him or her by saying: "May our Lord and God, Jesus Christ, through the grace and bounties of his love towards mankind, forgive you all your transgressions. And I, his unworthy priest, through the power given to me by Him, do forgive and absolve you from all your sins, in the name of the Father, and of the Son, and of the Holy Spirit."

- **Matrimony:** Is the sacrament in which a man and a woman bind themselves to each other as husband and wife for life. Their Christian marriage is meant to express the reality of the unbreakable and intimate union between Jesus Christ and the Church and between God and humanity. Roman Catholic teaching does not recognize divorce or allow divorced persons to remarry, unless the original "marriage" has been annulled—declared by church law to have been invalid. Eastern Orthodox Churches do not have annullments, but they do permit divorce in certain cases and allow divorced persons to remarry. This is understood as a concession to human weakness in situations when the first

marriage has definitively broken down and the divorced Christian seeks a "second chance" to live out a life of matrimonial communion. Eastern Catholic Churches, like the Roman Catholic Church, forbid divorce but they do grant annulments when the situation seems to warrant it.

- **Holy Orders:** Is the sacrament in which men chosen by the church are made deacons, priests, or bishops. The principal powers of the priesthood are those Christ gave his apostles, who were the first priests: to offer the holy Eucharist, forgive sins, administer the sacraments, and preach the gospel. Since the Lateran Council of 1123, Roman Catholic priests have not been permitted to marry. In the Eastern Churches, parish priests are allowed to marry.

■ *A celebration of the sacrament of matrimony by a couple, witnessed by a priest in the name of the Church, in Buenos Aires, Argentina.*

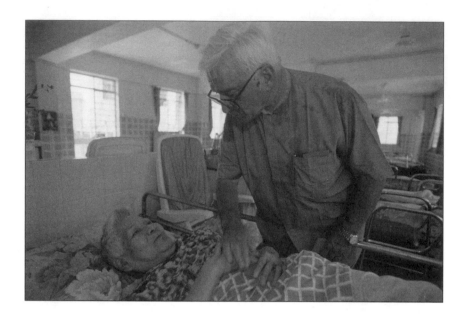

However, a candidate may only marry prior to his ordination to the priesthood or diaconate, and not afterwards. Only unmarried priests may become bishops in the Eastern Churches.

- **Anointing of the Sick:** Is a sacrament that gives the healing touch of Christ to an ill or suffering person. It is intended to bring strength to those who have been weakened by sickness, suffering, or old age. Both the Catholic and Eastern Orthodox Churches confer this sacrament on their faithful.

Church Organization

At the present time, church organization is the area which most divides the Roman Catholic Church and the Eastern Orthodox Churches. The major point of division is the role of the pope. Roman Catholics believe that the pope is the representative of Christ on earth and thus the leader of the worldwide Church. The Eastern Orthodox Churches recognize that the pope, the bishop of Rome, has a special role in relation to all the churches of the world. However, they believe that this means he should be honored above all the other bishops, not that he can exercise direct authority over all the churches of the world. Because of this difference in understanding the role of the pope, the Eastern Orthodox Churches are not in communion with the pope and the Roman Catholic Church. This means that they do not recognize themselves as part of the Roman Catholic Church. On the other hand, Eastern Catholic Churches are those churches which follow the Eastern traditions and liturgy, but are in communion with the Roman Catholic Church. Eastern Catholic Christians pray for the pope during the Divine Liturgy and do consider themselves to be part of the Catholic Church.

Despite these differences, there are still many similarities between Roman Catholics and Eastern Christians with regard to church organization. The most important principle is that of apostolic succession. Both Roman and Eastern Churches believe that the teaching of the apostles and the power that Christ conferred upon his apostles has been handed down in their churches through the succession of bishops that goes back to the earliest days of the church, the time when Christ's apostles lived. Although the Eastern Orthodox Catholic Churches are not part of the Roman Catholic Church, the Catholic Church recognizes the apostolic succession of the Eastern Orthodox Churches and considers the sacraments of the Eastern Orthodox Churches to be valid. It is the belief of Catholics and Eastern Orthodox Christians that the hierarchy of the church is necessary to maintain the constant teaching of Christ and his apostles. Tradition plays a very important role in Catholic and Orthodox Churches.

Roman Catholic Church Organization

The hierarchy of the Catholic Church has three levels: the pope, who is the bishop of Rome and the spiritual leader of the worldwide Church; bishops, who are responsible for a diocese, or territorial district; and pastors, who are spiritual leaders of individual parishes. The pope appoints the bishops, who in turn appoint pastors.

Assisting the pope in governing the church are two bodies, the college of cardinals and the Roman curia.

• The college of cardinals is a group of Catholics, most often clergymen, appointed by the pope to serve as his advisers. They have the responsibility of electing a new pope when necessary.

- The Roman curia serves as the pope's administrative arm. It consists of the secretariat of state, which assists the pope most directly in both governing the church and communicating with the rest of the curia, and a number of other departments, each of which has a specific function.

Roman Catholics believe that the pope is infallible, or not able to err, in matters of faith and morals. This belief is based on the understanding that the Church is guided by the presence of Christ and protected by the Holy Spirit from error. Roman Catholics believe that this protection of the Church from error takes place in the teachings of the pope when he speaks *ex cathedra*, or by virtue of his office. The pope does not have infallibility, or the inability to err, in connection with other aspects of church affairs, but he does have absolute authority. He is considered the highest teacher, judge, and governing power in the Church.

The pope is the ruler of Vatican City, an independent state within the city of Rome, Italy. The Vatican has its own flag, coins, stamps, and public works. As an independent state, it has diplomatic status, and the pope sends representatives to other countries and receives ambassadors from them.

The governing power of the Church over its members is twofold. It has a legislative, or lawmaking role, and a judicial role pertaining to the administration of church law. Church laws regulate the conduct of the Church and its members. Church courts make decisions in matters pertaining to church law. The chief role of the Church, however, is not to judge but to teach and exhort through its teaching. It is in few cases that the Church deals with its members through any official legal system; generally it instructs through teaching and exhortation.

Eastern Orthodox Church Organization

The Eastern Orthodox Churches are the major churches in Greece, Russia, eastern Europe, western Asia, and much of the

Middle East. Individually, they are usually called by their national names, such as the Greek Orthodox Church or the Russian Orthodox Church, but they are united by common beliefs and traditions. Most of the Orthodox Churches in the United States are governed by the hierarchy of the country from which that church originated. For example, the Antiochian Orthodox Church is ultimately governed by the Antiochian Church in Syria, although it does have bishops in the United States. Early in the 20th century, an attempt was made to unite all the Orthodox Churches in the United States as a self-governing American Church. This became the Orthodox Church of America, which was founded in 1970. However, this attempt did not succeed in uniting all the churches. Nevertheless, Orthodox Christians in America continue to work for a unified Orthodox American Church.

■ *Cardinal Law of Boston and Cardinal Maradiaga of Honduras discuss church issues concerning Central America.*

■ *His Holiness Abune Paulos, Patriarch of Eritrea, in formal ecclesiastical attire.*

Among the self-governing Churches, those of Constantinople, Alexandria, Antioch, and Jerusalem hold special places of honor in Eastern Orthodoxy for historical reasons. The greatest honor is given to the leader of the Church of Constantinople, who is called the ecumenical patriarch. His is a primacy of honor, and not of direct authority over all the Eastern Orthodox Churches of the world. All the Eastern Orthodox Churches pray for the ecumenical patriarch of Constantinople during the Divine Liturgy, just as Roman Catholics express their communion with the pope by praying for him during Mass. There are also some Orthodox Churches, the Oriental Orthodox Churches, who do not recognize the primacy of honor of the patriarch of Constantinople. These are the Churches, such as the allegedly Monophysite Churches of the patriarchates of Alexandria and Antioch, who disagreed with the declaration of the Council of Chalcedon in 451. The Oriental Orthodox Churches maintain good relations with the Eastern Orthodox Churches and now generally agree that the doctrinal conflict was caused by a misunderstanding that was likely due to imprecise language and thus does not indicate a real difference of belief. According to this conciliatory interpretation of the ancient doctrinal conflict, all Orthodox Churches hold that Christ is both God and man.

The three major orders of Orthodox clergy are the bishops, priests, and deacons. The two minor orders are the subdeacons and readers. Deacons, subdeacons, and readers assist the priest during religious services. Both the spiritual life and the administration of the churches are governed by the principle of shared responsibility between the clergy and the laity, or nonclergy. The laity often take part in the administration of their church and in the election of their clergy.

Eastern Catholic Church Organization

Eastern Catholic Churches are united with Rome, but their organizational structures parallel those of the various Eastern Orthodox Churches. This is to be expected, since these Eastern Catholic Churches are churches that have their origins in the same parts of the world as the Eastern Orthodox Churches and have the same liturgy and traditions as their Eastern Orthodox counterparts. The main organizational difference, however, is that they elected to resume communion with the pope of Rome. These Churches each have their own head, or patriarch. The internal affairs of each Eastern Catholic Church are usually decided by the patriarch of that church and its bishops. The largest Eastern Catholic Churches in the United States are the Melkite Church and the Maronite Church, which originate in the Middle East, and the Ukrainian and Ruthenian Churches, which are Slavic in their origins.

Whether in the Roman Catholic or in the Eastern Catholic Churches, church organization is not considered to be exclusively a matter of administration and government. It is viewed as an ordering that is directed by the Holy Spirit for the maintenance of the Church in the teachings of Jesus Christ. Such a spiritual view of organization is based on the words of Christ at the end of Matthew's Gospel: "And remember, I am with you always, to the end of the age." (Matt. 28.20)

CHAPTER **5**

The Influence of the Catholic and Orthodox Churches

*T*hroughout its history, the Catholic Church has had an impact in many areas of human life in the lands where it has been practiced. The extent of its influence has been greater or less in different countries at various times, but its influence was strongly felt in Europe during the Middle Ages, or as it is sometimes called, the Age of Faith.

Comparatively, the influence of Catholicism, as with many forms of religion, has diminished in recent years, causing some Catholics to believe that today's world is too secular, or non-religious. Yet, even today the influence of the Catholic Church is strong. There is hardly a town in the United States that does not have at least one Catholic church. Many architecturally striking buildings in American and European cities are the Roman Catholic cathedrals. Catholic schools are recognized for the educational contributions that they have made to American society. Moreover, politicians and pollsters alike are very aware of the power of the so-called "Catholic vote."

What follows is a concise survey of the influence of the Catholic Church on daily life, education, art, architecture, music, and literature in the United States and around the world.

Daily Life

In an early chapter of the Acts of the Apostles, Luke states that the followers of Christ continued to gather in Jerusalem and that they shared their belongings with one another. "They would sell their possessions and goods and distribute the proceeds to all, as any had need." (Acts 2.45). During the earliest days of the Church, Christians must not have stood out that much from other Jews who followed a particular teacher. They went to the synagogue, and dressed like the other Jews. They celebrated the sabbath and religious feasts, even though they were beginning to give them new Christian meanings or interpretations.

As the Church spread among the Greek and other non-Jewish communities, Christ's followers were also not noticeably different from the rest of their fellow countrymen. Christians were not identified by peculiar customs or a particular language that set them apart from their neighbors. Rather, Christ's followers were found among non-Christians in various countries, and they lived life very much as it was lived by other citizens. Yet, Christians throughout the ages have tried to point out what makes them different from other people. Their special calling is to imitate God's love. Many religions demand that their followers love God with all their heart and soul and love their neighbors as they love themselves. The special approach of Christian love is stated in the First Letter of Saint John: "In this way the love of God was revealed to us: God sent his only Son into the world so that we might have life through him. In this is love: not that we have loved God, but that he loved us and sent his Son as expiation for our sins. Beloved, since God has so loved us, we also must love one another." (1 John 4.9–11).

Love, as Catholic Christians envision it, cannot be something true Christians engage in just on Sundays and forget about during the rest of the week. Nor is it measured in terms of loving someone because he or she returns that love. According to Catholics, God's love for people is not conditional on their reciprocal love. He loves us simply, unconditionally. That is the model of love he sets for his people. Christians see the life and death of God in Jesus Christ as inaugurating a new kingdom in which the ethics of unconditional love permeates all existence.

The celebration of the Sunday Eucharist (sometimes called the "love-feast" in the early Church) is considered as an exemplary model of the communion that all people are meant to experience not only with God but also with each other. One of the Eastern fathers of the Church, Saint John Chrysostom (c.347–407), insisted that just as all Christians participate equally in the Eucharist of Christ, they should work for the equal sharing of all worldly goods. In a similar spirit, the Catholic philosopher Blaise Pascal (1623–1662) is reported to have invited poor people into his house for a meal when he was too sick to attend the Eucharist in Church.

In the United States today, Catholics generally practice their religion without much fanfare. They practice their faith in the atmosphere of their families, or in church on Sunday. In the Eastern Catholic tradition, the customary Lenten fast is to

■ *A first communion procession through the town of Positano, Italy to the Duomo (Cathedral) Square.*

abstain from meat and dairy products for the entire 40 days of Lent, though sometimes modifications of this tradition are allowed. Special Lenten services in the Eastern Rite are observed two or three times a week and every day during the climactic "Holy Week" that extends from Palm Sunday to Easter Sunday. Religious services are also held on important Catholic feast days, such as Easter and Christmas. Most Catholics, however, live their visible lives in the same way as other citizens. They wear no special clothing and rarely follow any special dietary regulations. Some children may attend parochial, or church-run, schools, but many also attend public schools. For the most part, there is no significant difference between the Catholic population and the general population in the life they live.

A few Catholic communities, because of their particular dedication to the Gospel teachings, do live quite differently from their neighbors. Catholic priests, monks, and nuns at times have worn distinctive dress within and outside their religious houses. These distinctive garments were meant to set them apart as a group whose members were in a special way committed to dedicating their lives to God. Unlike these special groups, however, most Christians dress in the various styles of the times, in no way reflecting their religious beliefs.

Education

Christ's first apostles were not scholars. They were fishermen. Christ did not suggest that scholars were particularly qualified to preach the Gospel. Some early Christians, such as Tertullian in the early 3rd century, preferred a Christianity that was characterized by the simplicity of the fisherman rather than by the intellectual investigation of the scholar. While Tertullian himself was a highly educated person, he wished to employ his intellectual talents in the service of the simplicity of the Gospel and was afraid that the worldly wisdom of his time would undermine Christian teachings. For example, the schools of the classical world of Greece and Rome used for their basic texts the works of writers such as Homer and Virgil, with their tales of vengeful gods and stories of heroes who seemed to be centered upon their own achievements. There were in fact many reasons

for Christians to become anti-intellectual, since the early Greek and Roman intellectual worlds, from a Christian perspective, offered such poor examples to follow.

Yet, many resisted this temptation. Justin Martyr (c.100–c.163) realized that his search for life's meaning through the study of pagan classics was not satisfying. He was looking for something more than these classics provided, and so he turned to the study of the Gospels.

Other Christians found the teachings of the Gospels to be misunderstood or misrepresented by opponents. They realized that they needed skills in logic and rhetoric to disprove them. Thus, Christians saw the need for studying the traditional subjects of the seven liberal arts that the ancient Greeks and Romans studied—grammar, rhetoric, dialectic, arithmetic, geometry, music, and astronomy—to defend and explain the teachings of the Gospels. Saint Augustine, in his work *On Christian Teaching*,

■ *The Church of St. Apollonaris in Ravenna, Italy, offers one of the earliest mosaics in the Latin Christian world. This particular work represents Jesus Christ as the Good Shepherd caring for his spiritual sheep. It is through mosaics and stained glass windows that many Christians learned the lessons of the Scriptures.*

A nun from the Daughters of St. Paul uses a mixing board to produce the latest educational materials.

argued strongly that these studies were key to understanding, explaining, and defending the biblical writings.

It was not, however, a matter of simply learning the same subjects as were taught in the non-Christian schools. There was the need to develop the kind of learning that would be properly Christian. This task involved the development of a Christian language. Saint Clement of Alexandria (c.150–220) employed a famous image to illustrate this effort: the new song of the divine Word demanded new words. There were no words for the Christian God who is three persons. Words like "Trinity" or "Triune God" had to be coined by Christians to express the special character of their God. The same was true of Jesus Christ, that is, God the Son who took on human flesh. To express the reality of Christ, their Redeemer, Christians had to invent the word "Savior." When Christians invented words like "Savior," non-Christian grammarians must have ridiculed their new word. Saint Augustine, in one of his sermons, tells his audience not to worry about the laughter of the grammarians. Christians should rather focus on how true the new expression is. Before the coming of Christ, he notes, there was no Savior, so people who were not Christians did not have a word for a reality that did not exist for them.

Often, however, there were words available, but Christians had to give them new meanings. There was a Greek word "catechumenus," which meant "learner." The Christians gave it a new meaning: "Someone who is learning about the Christian faith."

The word "pagan" was a military term that referred to those who were civilians and not soldiers. For Christians, "a pagan" was a person who was not a soldier of Christ. Very many words for Christians had to take on new meanings or had to be invented. Christian education had many challenges to face, and it took a great deal of effort to develop Christian language and meaning within schools that were "pagan." Eventually, they developed their own schools.

Schools, attached to monasteries and cathedrals, were built to educate people who did not intend to pursue church positions. As more towns were established and more cathedrals were built, these schools increased in number throughout Europe, especially in France. Many of the major universities of Europe developed from such schools. The Roman Catholic Church, as part of its own reform movement in the 16th and 17th centuries, also expanded its educational activities. Schools were established for Catholic children in which they were taught in their own languages.

In the Eastern Christian tradition, anti-intellectualism never gained a strong footing. Eastern theologians, such as Saints Basil the Great (c.329–379), Gregory of Nyssa (c.330–c.395), and Gregory Nazianzen (c.329–390), tended to be highly versed in the knowledge of their time. Saint Basil (c.330–379) is especially well-known for his essay written to adolescents encouraging them to read the Greek classics, since Christians cannot afford to be unlettered. For another Eastern Christian theologian, Saint Maximos the Confessor (c.580–622), knowledge— not just moral discipline—was an important step in the Christian's progress in the spiritual life. In modern times, we can again point to the example of the popular Russian priest Father Alexander Men (1935–1990) who saw all human culture as a valuable witness to humanity's search for God, a search fulfilled in the divine-human person of Jesus Christ.

Most immigrants who came to the Americas from Europe set up the kinds of schools they had known in their homelands. Saint Elizabeth Bayley Seton (1774–1821), founder of the American Sisters of Charity, was the architect of the parochial school system in the United States. She received her inspiration from the training established in France by Louise de Marillac (1591–1660), the co-founder of the Sisters of Charity. Under such inspiration, Catholics established and supported their own schools. Most of these were elementary schools where reading, writing, and religion were taught. Later, secondary schools and even small colleges were founded by churches, primarily to train young men for the ministry. Many of these colleges have developed in the 20th century into large and respected universities.

Art and Architecture

Although the Christian church did not continue many of the ritual laws of the Jewish people, they did cling to the Ten Commandments. The first commandment prohibits the making of images of anything in heaven or on earth that could serve as an idol. This prohibition made the early Christians hesitate to create any images at all. The earliest works of Christian art began appearing in the 3rd century in the form of mural paintings in burial chambers, such as the Roman catacombs. The subjects of these paintings included Christ's early miracle of the multiplication of the loaves and fishes and scenes based on other Biblical stories.

As the Church came out of hiding in the 4th century, after years of persecution, works of Christian art began to appear. This can be seen in the beautiful mosaics that survive in the Church of San Vitale of Ravenna, Italy, or in the Cathedral of Monreale in Sicily, or in the illuminations (special ornamental illustrations) found in early manuscripts of the Vatican library. Before monarchs, lords, and wealthy merchants began to patronize artists during the Renaissance, almost all art was religious art, commissioned by and for the Church. By the 500s, a distinct style of art and architecture had developed in the Byzantine Empire. In the domed churches of Byzantium, tapestries, mosaics, paintings, and murals recounting the life of Christ and the careers of saints and martyrs adorned every surface. Remnants of this form of art remain in Eastern Catholic Churches. It is also visible in the Basilica of Saint Mark in Venice, Italy, where both the architecture and the mosaics reveal the presence of Venice's ancient links to Byzantium.

The Middle Ages in Europe was a period of deep religious faith. The Church became the period's most influential patron of the arts, building churches and monasteries, decorating them with paintings, and filling them with altars, candelabra, and screens made of wood or iron. The frescoes, or paintings on fresch plaster, of the 14th century Italian painter Giotto (c.1266–1337) and the stained glass of Chartres Cathedral, in France, for example, are visible reminders of this age of glory for Christian art.

The Medieval and Renaissance periods also saw the flourishing of the great Byzantine tradition of making icons. From

■ *Hagia Sophia, the Church of Divine Wisdom, at Istanbul, Turkey, is a masterpiece of Byzantine architecture dating from the 6th century.*

■ *Sainte Chapelle in Paris shows the glories of Gothic stained glass to its constant stream of visitors.*

this period, we have two of the most beloved icons in the Eastern tradition. One of these is "The Vladimir Madonna," also known as "The Mother of Loving Kindness," which depicts a tender embrace between the Virgin Mary and the child Jesus. It was painted in the 12th century and presented as a gift honoring Prince Vladimir of Russia (c.956–1015) by the patriarch of Constantinople. The other is known as "The Old Testament Trinity" or "The Hospitality of Abraham and Sarah," which presents the angels who visit Abraham and Sarah, according to the Old Testament account, as a symbol of the Triune God. The icon was painted by one of the great Byzantine painters, Andrei Rublev (c.1360–1430), in the 15th century.

Architects in the early part of the Middle Ages built churches modeled after Rome's great buildings. This Romanesque architecture, however, took on fresh creative forms. The more definitively Christian form of architecture is found later in the Middle Ages with the development of Gothic cathedrals, such as the Cathedral of Notre Dame in France, or Cologne Cathedral in Germany, with arches and towers that seem to soar to heaven. These cathedrals were intended to inspire a mood of reverence among worshipers, lifting their hearts to the heavens above. The invention of supports for the soaring walls of the cathedral freed them for windows. Magnificent stained glass windows became the principal form of internal decoration in these cathedrals. As they knelt before richly carved altars, surrounded by beautiful images, bathed in colored light that had filtered through the stained glass windows, medieval worshipers must have felt both awed and uplifted.

Even though much art during the Renaissance, the 15th and 16th century revival of Greek and Roman artistic forms, began to be sponsored by non-church patrons, and increasingly artists were creating paintings and sculptures for private enjoyment, still some of the greatest works of religious art were created during this period. Pope Julius II (1503–1513) made Rome an important artistic center. Among the works of art he commissioned was the painting of the ceiling of the Sistine Chapel in the Vatican by Michelangelo (1475–1564). Other famous artists of the time included Raphael (1483–1520), renowned for "The

Marriage of the Virgin" and "The Transfiguration" and Leonardo da Vinci (1452–1519), best known for "The Last Supper."

During the Protestant Reformation, the Catholic Church attempted at times to counter the charges of immorality and idolatry that were launched by the reformers. Church painting was more strictly regulated. Pope Pius V (1566–1572) went so far as to order clothing added to the figures Michelangelo had painted in the Sistine Chapel.

However, the art and architecture of Eastern Christendom was relatively unaffected by these movements of Reformation and Counter-Reformation. Eastern Churches continued to be built in the classic Byzantine style. They also were adorned with icons, especially on the iconostasis, or screen that stands between the congregation and the sanctuary with its altar. Eastern Catholics likewise continued these architectural practices. For them, as well as for the Orthodox, such features were not simply ornamental but aided their understanding of the Church as a concrete manifestation of the kingdom of God and the communion of saints.

Music

Christianity played an important part in the early growth of classical music. However, this was not the first influence Christianity had on music. The oldest known Christian form of music was plainsong, a simple form of vocal music that was used in early Catholic Church services. Plainsong was so called because a soloist or choir sang the melody without instrumental accompaniment or harmony. Plainsong developed gradually from early Jewish religious music, and much of it was set to the words of the Psalms, lyrical poems from the Old Testament. The most important type of plainsong was Gregorian chant, developed during the reign of Pope Gregory I (590–604). In the early Middle Ages, music was almost entirely in the service of the liturgy or public worship of the Church.

For the Eastern Church, music began to play an increasing role in the liturgy during the period of the Byzantine Empire, from about the 4th to the 15th century. About the end of the 5th

■ *A plainsong page from a manuscript illuminated by Bartholomeo di Fruosino in the 14th century. The words say, "My sins, O Lord, are inbedded in me like arrows, but the wounds...."*

century, Romanus (490–556), a Greek monk, composed the words and music of hymns that still form part of the Byzantine liturgy. Musical expression has always been a prominent feature of the Eastern Christian tradition. To this day, the Byzantine liturgy is for the most part sung rather than recited. Eastern Christians give great honor to the early poet-theologians who penned many of the traditional hymns. These hymns emphasize central aspects of the Christian faith. The haunting melancholy chant that commemorates the crucifixion of Christ exemplifies this style:

Today he who hung the earth upon the waters
   is hung upon a tree
The King of the angels is adorned with a crown
   of thorns
He who wraps the heavens with clouds is wrapped
   with the purple of mockery
He who set Adam free…receives blows upon his face
The Bridegroom of the Church is pierced through
   with nails
The Son of the Virgin is stabbed with a spear
We venerate your Passion, O Christ,
Show us also your glorious Resurrection.

For the most part, in the Eastern tradition such chants are normally sung without any instrumental accompaniment. Eastern Christians hold that the most fitting instrument to use in liturgical worship is the human voice, since Christians believe that the human being was created in the image of God. A slight exception to this rule is the use of cymbals in the Coptic (Egyptian) tradition. Of the two main styles of Eastern Christian music, the Greek and the Russian, the former tends to be simpler and more rhythmic, while the latter is more elaborate and makes greater use of harmony. The Russian style reached a high point of harmonic complexity and richness in the High Renaissance and Baroque periods.

Since the 19th century, liturgical and devotional music has been composed by some of the great Russian composers. High points within this tradition include the setting to music of the Liturgy of Saint John Chrysostom by Peter Tchaikovsky (1840–1893), as well as the Great Vespers of Sergei Rachmaninov (1873–1943). Other secular composers who also composed Byzantine choral music are Pavel Chesnokov (1877–1944), Dimitri Bortniansky (1751–1825), and Igor Stravinsky (1882–1971). Stravinsky is well-known in the West for his "Firebird Suite" and

"The Rite of Spring," but is equally well-known in Slavic lands for his musical rendering of the "Our Father" and for other liturgical music.

In the Western tradition, an Italian Benedictine monk named Guido d'Arezzo (c.995–c.1049) revolutionized the teaching of music during the 11th century. He introduced the four-line staff and is credited with establising the first six notes of the scale. These achievements made the teaching of music much easier. Another great musical innovation of the 11th century was polyphony—the putting together of two or more voices harmoniously. In the 1300s, the French composer Guillaume de Machaut (1300–1377) wrote the first polyphonic Catholic Mass.

Many forms of classical music were created for Church services. Most choral music in particular has been written for religious ceremonies. The principal form of such choral music is the Mass, a series of pieces composed for a Catholic worship service. The earliest Masses were written for small, unaccompanied choruses. Only later did polyphonic Masses develop, at times accompanied by instruments. The requiem, which is a special Mass composed for funerals, also frequently involves choral singing. Requiems have been written by such composers as Wolfgang Amadeus Mozart (1756–1791), Louis Hector Berlioz (1803–1869), and Guiseppe Verdi (1813–1901).

A hymn is a song of praise, and most hymns glorify God. Since biblical times, Jews have used the Psalms of the Old Testament as hymns. Today, both Jews and Christians sing hymns during their religious services. Until the 1500s, most Christian hymns were sung in Latin. In recent years, many of these Latin hymns have been rewritten in vernacular, or local language, forms. They have also been joined by a completely new collection of hymns supported by guitars. These hymns have very much been developed to encourage a more active musical participation by the whole community of worshipers.

Literature

From the 3rd century, Christian authors, such as Tertullian (160–230), Saint John Chrysostom (c.347–407), and Saint Augustine (354–430), are still widely considered by classical scholars to be among the finest stylists of classical Greek and Latin, respectively. In the West, it was as the language of the Church—no longer of the Roman Empire—that Latin was to remain alive and vigorous up to the end of the Middle Ages.

After the fall of Rome, many European monasteries were founded that preserved Christianity and classical learning. Monastery libraries contained not only Bibles, biblical commentaries, and liturgical books, but also the classics of ancient Greece and Rome that otherwise would have been lost forever. Monasteries also fostered the emergence of literature in the vernacular, as opposed to Latin. These libraries with their faithful copies of texts provided the raw materials that later would form the basis of Charlemagne's (c.742–814) educational reforms.

A wealth of literature was produced from the beginning of the 5th to the 17th century in Europe, and many of the most admired works were written by Catholic authors. Although some of these works, such as the records of monasteries compiled by Christian monks during the Middle Ages, were merely histories of monastic foundations; others, such as the *Ecclesiastical History of the English Nation* written by a British monk called the Venerable Bede (673–735), were masterpieces. Bede wrote many works on science, grammar, history, and theology.

In the Christian East, the same period saw the flourishing of literature that dealt with progress in the spiritual life. Among the most important writers of the period were Saint John Climacus (525–606), whose *Ladder of Divine Ascent* is considered a classic of Eastern Catholic spirituality, and Saint Symeon the New Theologian (949–1022) whose experiences of God as "divine fire" are based on the scene of Jesus' transfiguration before his disciples in the Gospel accounts.

One of the most celebrated classics of early English literature, Geoffrey Chaucer's (c.1340–1400) *Canterbury Tales*, came out of the medieval tradition of pilgrimages, journeys made by people of diverse backgrounds to sacred places. Chaucer's tales relate the adventures of a group of pilgrims on their way to the shrine in Canterbury of the murdered archbishop Thomas à Becket.

In Eastern Christendom, the 18th century saw the publication of the monumental *Philokalia*, an anthology of spiritual literature derived from authors who lived from the 4th to the 15th century. This classic work quickly became a handbook of Eastern Christian spirituality both for monks and ordinary Christians. It was compiled by Saint Nicodemus of the Holy Mountain (1748–1809) and published in Venice in 1782.

In the 19th century, the Orthodox Christian culture of Russia gave rise to some of the most monumental classics of modern literature. Great Russian authors, such as Feodor Dostoyevsky (1821–1881) and Leo Tolstoy (1828–1910), were preoccupied with religious questions, and their major works deal directly with religious themes and treat them in a way that is explicitly Christian.

Catholic literature has continued to develop in the modern and contemporary period and has done so in many forms. Theological and philosophical themes have been elaborated in the writings of Jacques Maritain (1882–1973), Etienne Gilson, Teilhard de Chardin, and Gabriel Marcel (1889–1973). The novels of Graham Greene (1904–1991) have often wrestled with the moral dilemmas facing Catholics in the contemporary world, and the works of Flannery O'Connor (1925–1964) have often treated themes challenging Catholics and many other religious people today.

Theater

Catholicism's influence on the theater was at first negative. In Rome, many forms of theater were popular—tragedy, comedy, farce, and pantomime. Most of these performances were offensive to the early Christians, however, and as Christianity grew more powerful, the Roman theater declined. In the 400s, actors were excommunicated, or denied participation in church functions, and Roman theater came to an end not long afterward. The last known theatrical performance in ancient Rome was in 533.

At the same time, Christian worship itself increasingly acquired a dramatic form. This development began in the Christian East as the Byzantine liturgy admitted a number of processions within the liturgy. Increasingly, the Eucharistic Liturgy came to be interpreted as a "drama" that reenacted the

■ *Actors rehearse a scene from the "Passion Play" at Oberammergau, a 350-year-old tradition in this mountain town south of Munich, Germany.*

life and death of Jesus. Byzantine hymns also developed a more dramatic form, consisting of dialogues between various figures in the Gospel narrative. A Christmas hymn, for example, would consist of a chanted conversation between Mary, Joseph, the angels, and the shepherds. The Passion of Christ often was sung by a large cast joined by the surrounding mob.

The rebirth of drama in the Roman Catholic Church began in the 900s when priests and choirboys began to act out short plays as part of the worship service, especially in the Church's attempt to make the Gospels "come alive." A large body of plays grew up around the Resurrection, the Christmas story, and other biblical events. The language of these plays was the language of the Church: Latin.

- **Mystery Plays:** In the 1300s, plays moved outdoors and began to be produced and acted by non-religious organizations, such as craft or trade organizations called guilds. The plays came to be called mystery plays from another name for these guilds: masteries or mysteries.

  Mystery plays were staged outdoors on large carts called pageant wagons. A wagon was drawn through a town to various places where spectators stood in the street or watched from nearby houses. The actors were townspeople, most of whom belonged to the guilds that produced the plays. Mystery plays were presented in cycles of several related dramas over a period of one or two days. Each guild in a town was responsible for one episode or play.

- **Miracle Plays:** Miracle plays, which developed out of mystery plays, were also popular during the Middle Ages. Like mystery plays, they were presented initially as part of Catholic Church services but lost the approval of the Church. After being driven out of the churches and into the streets, miracle plays were performed by trade guild members on feast days. Miracle plays dramatized events from the life of the Virgin Mary or the lives of saints. The action of most of these plays reached a climax in a miracle performed by the saint—which gave these plays their name.

- **Morality Plays:** Another form of medieval drama, the morality play, was first produced in England in the 1400s. Like the mystery and miracle play, the morality play developed from religious pageants. Its purpose was to teach a lesson or to show the eternal struggle between good and evil for control of human beings. The morality play became more fully developed than other types of medieval drama, growing from a fairly simple religious play to a secular entertainment performed by professional companies of actors. While morality plays were primarily serious, the characters who represented evil were usually treated in a comical way to make the play more entertaining to the audience. The clowns and fools in the plays of William Shakespeare (1564–1616) developed out of the comic characters in morality plays. *Everyman*, a favorite morality play of the 1500s, is still performed annually at a music and drama festival in Salzburg, Austria.

In Spain during the Middle Ages, drama became an important vehicle of religious teaching. Spanish religious plays combined elements of the mystery play and the morality play. Human and supernatural characters mingled with symbolic figures, such as Grace, Pleasure, and Sin. Dramatists borrowed their stories from both secular and religious sources, adapting them to uphold church teachings. Like the English mystery plays, the Spanish plays were performed outdoors on wagons.

During the late Middle Ages, European townspeople and villagers often staged Passion plays. These were performances which depicted the suffering, crucifixion, and death of Jesus Christ. By taking part in a Passion play, townspeople also participated in the drama of Christ's last days on earth. The Passion play tradition continues to the present in towns in southern Germany, western Austria, and Switzerland. The most famous one is held every ten years in the Bavarian town of Oberammergau.

In modern times, biblical themes and stories continue to be used as material in the creation of theatrical productions and movies. One contemporary example is a series of films, *The Decalogue*, based on the biblical Ten Commandments, by acclaimed Polish director Krzysztof Kieslowski (1941–1996). In these films, dramatic situations are created in modern settings in ways that explore the themes of the Ten Commandments. Anyone who is familiar with biblical lore will find that in these films the history of music, art, and literature throughout the course of Western civilization is permeated with explicit references to the resources of the Christian tradition.

CHAPTER 6

Catholicism and Orthodox Christianity Facing New Challenges

Christians have had to meet many challenges since the time of Christ and the apostles. They faced rejection by the Jewish community as the chief priests realized that the early Christians were not just followers of another charismatic teacher of their Jewish religious tradition, but of a person whom they considered the Son of God. The Church encountered persecution from the Romans, who thought of Christians as citizens of another kingdom and thus opposed to (or at least not supportive of) the Roman kingdom.

Pope Gregory the Great later pointed to challenges within the Church itself, posed by false or disturbing teachings, when he urged: "Let him who would speak wisely exercise great care, lest by his speech he disrupt the unity of his listeners." As time went on, this Catholic unity was greatly disturbed: first, by the Great Schism that split the Eastern and the Western Churches and that has kept the Catholic and the Orthodox Churches apart for almost a millennium; and then by the Reformation, which over the years gradually resulted in the formation of many Protestant sects, or churches, each united by certain shared beliefs and practices.

Ecumenism

One effort to overcome the long-lasting consequences of the separation of the Orthodox Churches from Rome and the divisive effects of the Protestant Reformation was to promote common Christian efforts to foster church-unity. This movement is called the *ecumenical* (meaning "worldwide") movement for Christian unity. Christians commonly recognize that their lack of unity is a painful contradiction to the witness of love entrusted to those who believe in Jesus Christ. Eastern Christians and Roman Catholics also recognize that the great similarities between their traditions make it a priority for each to seek union with the other. At the same time, both communities are in dialogue with other Christian Churches.

At the international level, the World Council of Churches was formed in Amsterdam, the Netherlands, in 1948. This is one forum for the various churches to dialogue with one another, with the goal of seeking reunification. The Roman Catholic Church did not become a member of this Council, preferring to carry out individual dialogues with particular churches. Some Orthodox Churches have chosen to join the World Council. The Church of Constantinople, which is the most influential among the Orthodox Churches, is a member of this Council and participates in all its deliberations. Like the Roman Catholic Church, however, other Orthodox Churches have chosen not to participate in this forum. They believe that the ecumenical movement presents the danger of implying that all beliefs and churches are equal, a principle with which the Roman Catholic Church and these Orthodox Churches would not agree.

While there have been efforts to heal the rift between divided Christians since the time of these divisions, these efforts have intensified in the 20th century. In the early part of the century many Catholic parishes in the United States dedicated a week of prayer for the promotion of unity among the various Christian Churches. During this week, called "The Church Unity Octave," sermons or lectures were given to inform Catholics about other Christian Churches, their beliefs and practices. The Catholic Church began to take an even more active part in the ecumenical movement in the 1960s. The Second Vatican Council (1962–1965), a worldwide council of Catholic Church leaders, passed a *Decree on Ecumenism*. This pledged the Catholic Church to work for the unity of all Christianity and encouraged Roman Catholics to take part in this ecumenical movement. The decree also permitted Catholics to join non-Catholics in common prayer, with the permission of the local bishops.

The Roman Catholic and Eastern Orthodox Dialogue

In 1965, the Roman Catholic Church also took a step toward ending the divisions between itself and Eastern Orthodox Churches. On December 7th of that year, Pope Paul VI (1963–1978) removed the sentence of excommunication, or exclusion from the rites of the church, on the patriarch of Constantinople that dated from 1054. The patriarch of Constantinople in turn removed a sentence of excommunication that the 11th-century patriarch had passed against a group of papal delegates. A decree of the Second Vatican Council also reaffirmed the equality of the rites of the Eastern and Western Churches. It recognized that the Eastern Orthodox Churches have valid sacraments and set forth circumstances under which Roman Catholics and Orthodox Christians could participate together in the sacraments and worship. Although the Roman Catholic Church allows Orthodox Christians under certain circumstances to participate in the Eucharistic liturgy of the Roman Catholic Church, the Orthodox Churches do not adopt the same policy toward Catholics. The rationale of the Catholic Church is that Orthodox Christians essentially share the same faith and the same sacraments; the Orthodox position is that participation in each other's sacraments is a sign of full unity and should not be engaged in before this unity is fully realized. The Roman Catholic Church does not allow Christians from any churches other than the Eastern Orthodox to participate in the sacraments of the Roman Catholic Church, due to the greater differences that exist in those cases.

Today, it is generally agreed that the major obstacle to the reunification of the Roman Catholic and Orthodox Churches is their different understandings of the role of the papacy. Roman Catholics believe that the pope is the center of unity for the worldwide Church and has the authority to rule over any part of the universal Church. They also believe that the pope has been granted the gift of speaking infallibly, or incapable of error, in matters of faith and doctrine, so that the Church may be guarded from serious error and departure from the Gospel message.

The Orthodox, on the other hand, believe that the pope is the first among bishops in the world and has a moral authority of honor that should be respected among all the world's churches. But they do not agree that the pope should directly govern all the churches of the world. The Orthodox also believe that the infallible teaching of the Church must be agreed upon in a universal gathering of bishops and not merely through the

■ *Pope John Paul II stopping in Greece on his way to the Holy Land. The pope, seen conversing with Archbishop Christodoulos, apologized for the brutality of the Crusaders who plundered Greek lands during their crusade in 1204.*

teaching of the pope. Pope John Paul II (1978–) has made it a priority of his pontificate to seek reunification with the Eastern Orthodox Churches. In a very important encyclical, *Ut Unum Sint* (which is Latin for "That all may be one") he has suggested that the Roman Catholic church is open to dialogue on the issue of the role of the papacy in order to arrive at a common understanding with the Orthodox Churches.

In May, 2001, after years of negotiations, the pope embarked on a pilgrimage to the Holy Land by retracing many of the steps that Saint Paul had taken on his journey from Palestine to Rome. This pilgrimage took him through much of the territory of the Eastern Orthodox Churches. The first stop was in Athens, where he delivered an apology for all the sins that Roman Catholics have committed against Orthodox Christians throughout the centuries. He apologized in particular for "the disastrous sack of the imperial city of Constantinople" by the crusaders in 1204. His visit, and the protests it drew from Orthodox clergy and laymen alike, made visible the deep wounds that still need to be healed before any serious union between Orthodox and Catholic Christians can be achieved. Pope John Paul II, however, has committed himself seriously to pursue the road to unity, and he has planned other journeys to this effect, most notably to Russia.

Lay Movements

The Second Vatican Council re-emphasized the role of lay people in the Catholic Church to overcome the misconception that the clergy is the only important element in the church. The laity, or lay people, are all those baptized Christians who have not been ordained to the threefold orders of the clergy. These orders are those of bishop, priest, and deacon. The role of the clergy is to administer the sacraments of the Church. The role of the laity is to transform the world through the power of Christ that is communicated by these sacraments. Thus, lay people are called to transform their lives, circumstances, and the realms of society in which they have direct participation in a way that is consistent with the message of the Gospel. One increasingly common Christian response has been the formation of Christian lay communities.

In the Roman Catholic Church, these lay communities have begun mostly in Europe during the years after the Second Vatican Council but have spread all over the world and are beginning to make their way into the United States. Usually, they include both lay people and priests. Lay people carry on their ordinary lives in family and work but meet together regularly for prayer and fellowship. Different communities have distinctive orientations. The Focolare movement, which began in Italy under the guidance of Chiara Lubich (1920–1998), is centered on the spirituality of being in unity with others through Christ. It has fostered much successful cooperation with members of other religions. The Community of Sant' Egidio, also started in Italy, has a special focus on solidarity with the poor and on peace-making. They serve those who are poor and have been successfully engaged in peace-making efforts in civil wars in Mozambique and Bosnia. More recently, similar groups have formed in the United States.

The Priesthood

The Second Vatican Council decree on the Ministry and Life of Priests reaffirmed the laws of celibacy, or not marrying, for Roman Catholic priests. It did permit Eastern Catholic priests to continue the Eastern Catholic and Orthodox practice that permits a married clergy.

A large number of Roman Catholic priests have left the priesthood and have married in recent years. In addition, the number of those preparing for the priesthood has dropped in many regions of the Roman Catholic world. These trends raise concerns that the time will come when there will not be enough priests to serve the Catholic faithful. The shortage of priests is more acute in rural areas, but is recently becoming more noticeable in the cities.

One solution for this problem might be to permit a married clergy. This is not an impossible solution, but other solutions would have to be exhausted before such a radical change would likely take place. Another solution suggested for this problem would be for women to be ordained as priests. Traditionally, women have been excluded from the Catholic priesthood. This

 A nun carries hosts and a chalice to women in a maternity clinic in Port au Prince, Haiti.

is a condition that exists to this day. The ordination of women in the Orthodox Churches has not yet become an issue for debate. The Catholic Church does not doubt a woman's ability to lead others, or to guide, or instruct. The Church's argument against the ordination of women is based on the Church's understanding of the Bible: the fact that Christ was masculine, and that he chose twelve male apostles to carry out his ministry. The Roman Catholic Church's position is clearly stated in the Vatican declaration Inter Insigniores (The Order of the Priesthood):

> *This practice of the Church therefore has a normative character; in fact of conferring priestly ordination only on men, it is a question of the unbroken tradition throughout the history of the Church, universal in the East and West, and alert to repress abuses immediately. This norm, based on Christ's example, has been and is still observed because it is considered to conform to God's plan for His Church.*

If a married priesthood and female priesthood are possible but unlikely solutions, then other solutions must be found to meet this challenge of a shortage of priests. Already, lay people have taken over many responsibilities that had traditionally been assumed by priests, even though they are duties not essential to the priestly office. Lay people now often have jurisdiction over parish buildings and their upkeep. Parochial assistants—religious men or women who are not ordained priests—organize parish activities, such as prayer groups, religious education discussions, parish reachout groups serving the poor, the sick, and the elderly. Special groups perform duties formerly carried out by pastors: bringing the Eucharist to the bedridden or counseling those seriously ill or near death. In many ways, the shortage of priests in many locales has offered opportunities for laymen and laywomen to discover callings they had never dreamed of before.

The Catholic Church's View on Human Sexuality

The 20th century has seen a significant change in people's attitudes toward sexuality. Many countries also have faced problems associated with population growth, such as overcrowding and the danger of spoiling or depleting many of the world's valuable natural resources. With the development of new birth control methods and the desire on the part of many people to limit the size of their families, new challenges have been posed to the traditional moral positions of the Catholic Church.

The Catholic Church views sex as something naturally good. The purpose of sex is to beget children, if God grants this benefit, and to foster mutual love. The official Church attitude is that the fostering of mutual love cannot by artificial means deliberately impede the natural purpose of sexual union: the begetting of children. With the fight against AIDS, this policy against birth control has become even more controversial, as it also forbids the use of condoms to protect against the contraction of HIV.

This teaching of the Church regarding sexuality has many ramifications. Sexual union of unmarried persons is forbidden, since they are not formally committed to one another through marriage and are not in a committed relationship to raise children, who would be expected naturally to follow from their sexual union. Adultery, or sexual union with a person who is married to someone else, is also forbidden for the same reasons. Homosexual unions are also prohibited since they cannot achieve the primary natural purpose of human sexuality, the begetting of children.

These teachings of the Church have received many challenges from those promoting birth or population control, from those claiming that people have a right to sex without the obligation to produce and care for children, and from those who wish to defend the freedom of choice as the true foundation of human dignity. The Catholic Church aims at defending the goodness and the high goals of human sexuality, the dignity of human love, the respect for human life, and the responsibilities associated with human's sexual nature. It recognizes the tendency of human individuals at times to care more about their sexual pleasure than to be concerned with avoiding the complex consequences of sexual activity that affects love relations with others and produces undesired offspring.

The Catholic Church's Position on Abortion

Like the issue of birth control, the issue of abortion has taken on grand proportions in the last decades of the 20th century, especially in America and many western European countries. The Second Vatican Council summarized the commitment of the Catholic Church to the welfare of the fetus, condemning abortion as an unspeakable crime and asking that the fetus be given the greatest care right from the moment of conception. Roman Catholic moral teaching does permit the invocation of the "principle of double effect" to argue that in certain extreme situations, such as a threat to the mother's life, the death of the fetus may be permitted (not chosen), because it is not the direct and willful taking of innocent life but rather the indirect result of saving the mother's life. But the Catholic Church explicitly denies women a right to choose to terminate an unwanted pregnancy, even in instances of rape or incest, placing a higher value on the life of the fetus than on any such right to choose by women.

Leo XIII (r.1878–1903), who enjoyed one of the longest papal reigns, dealt often with social issues that touched the daily lives of working people.

The Catholic Church and its Social Challenges

Urged on by Leo XIII's (1878–1903) social encyclical letters, the Catholic Church has met many of the social challenges that confront churches in the contemporary world. Especially in the United States, Catholic schools have helped poor immigrants and their children gain the educational background to advance in society. Catholic hospitals have for more than a century shown the corporal and spiritual "works of mercy" to the sick and dying and their families. Priests and Catholic lay people have played roles in the building of labor unions that brought workers better pay and better working conditions.

Liberation Theology

In South and Central America the interplay of politics and religion has been the focus of much attention since the time of the Second Vatican Council. The Council called on Catholics to be engaged in the modern world and its problems. The social situations in many South and Central American countries was such that 90 percent of the people were counted among the poor. In 1968, the Catholic bishops of South America called on all Catholics to become involved in social questions. They also declared that the Church should give special consideration to the poor.

In 1972, this call of the Catholic bishops found one of its expressions in Gustavo Guttierez's book, *A Theology of Liberation*. The work of this Peruvian priest began the movement called *liberation theology*. The chief characteristic of this movement is that it understands the Church's gospel message of freedom to be one that is interpreted in view of the experience of the poor and the oppressed who are enslaved in different ways, but especially by the social institutions under which they live. The leading teachers of this movement have been Leonardo (1938–) and Clodovis (1944–) Boff, Franciscan priests in Brazil, and Jon Sobrino (1938–), a Jesuit priest, in El Salvador. The liberation theology movement has had significant success in focusing attention on the plight of the poor and has pulled together efforts to alleviate their suffering.

Efforts at progress in improving the social lot of the poor in South and Central America have not always been peaceful. In 1998, Juan Gerardi, the auxiliary bishop of Guatermala City, was beaten to death two days after he published the war-crimes report, "Guatemala, Never Again." This report chronicled the war-crimes that have taken place during the 36 years of civil war in Guatemala.

In these efforts, the Church has moved into new and more delicate roles in different societies. Its judgments, discretion, prudence, and courage are tested in new and politically complicated ways. However, that it makes these efforts shows that the Catholic Church is still alive and active in the contemporary world, struggling with its economic, political, and social problems.

■ *Members of the el-Molo tribe attend Mass in Lolyangallani, Kenya.*

Problems Facing American Orthodox Churches Today

The Orthodox Churches in the United States have some special challenges of their own. The ethnic ties of the different Orthodox Churches makes it hard to form any kind of unity between the Churches that might be able to transcend national and political boundaries. Since the ethnic element is so strong in these diverse and separated Churches, as the younger generations become more Americanized, will it be possible to preserve its link to a Church that has strong ties to its ethnic tradition? In liturgical matters, will the ancient symbols and practices remain vital for the young who might well want to identify with America more than with an Orthodox Church with foreign roots? To meet these challenges, efforts have been made to introduce English into the Divine Liturgy and to update music; but still the traditions in these religious communities seem to be so strong that adaptation comes slowly.

Conclusion

The Catholic and Orthodox Churches have been attempting to meet the various challenges that have been presented by ancient religious disputes, by social concerns, and by modern secular ways of interpreting the value of religious organizations. In a world where a church is considered helpful to society by its social, moral, and political contributions, the chief challenge it faces seems to be the ability to continue to make these contributions and at the same time to convey the deeper beliefs and values which make it the Church founded by Christ. For the Catholic and Orthodox Churches, this latter challenge has always been present. Both communities of Christians believe, however, that they do not rely on their efforts alone. Christ has promised his followers his continual help, when he gave them their calling: "Go therefore and make disciples of all nations,…teaching them to obey everything that I have commanded you. And remember, I am with you always, to the end of the age." (Matt. 28.18–20)

GLOSSARY

Apostle—One of the twelve disciples chosen by Jesus (Matt. 2.4) or certain other early Christian leaders (Acts 14.14; Rom. 16.7; Gal 1.1).

Assyria—One of the strong Mediterranean civilizations that conquered the Jewish people in 731 B.C.E.

Babylonia—One of the conquering nations that overcame the Jewish people. They flourished in the Mesopotamian area and conquered the Jews in 586 B.C.E.

Baptism—Ceremony in which one enters the church family. It is a way of showing that you have been washed free of sin by the death and rising from the dead of Jesus Christ.

Basilica—A church, such as the Lateran Basilica, built according to an ancient Roman plan for a court of justice or a place of public assembly, with an oblong nave and a semicircular apse at one end.

Beatitudes—The blessings listed by Jesus in his Sermon on the Mount. They are considered the equivalent to the Ten Commandments of Moses or the expectations of the ideals to be pursued by Christians.

Catechism—A textbook regarding Christian beliefs and life used for preparing believers to accept the responsibilities of mature faith.

Charismatic—Gifted with charisma or spiritual grace, particularly one of the manifestations of the Holy Spirit, such as speaking in tongues.

Charismatic movements—A religious movement begun as Pentecostalism in the United States in 1901, that accentuates personal and direct experience of the Holy Spirit independently of sacraments and church institutions.

Chrism—Holy Oil blessed for confirmation and symbolizing the strength that is necessary for leading a mature Christian life and facing the challenges the call to Christian maturity brings.

Church—The people of God or those destined to inherit the kingdom of God.

Creed—A short statement of the basic beliefs of the Christian Church (e.g. the Apostles' Creed, the Athanasian Creed, and the Nicene Creed).

Ecumenical Council—A worldwide council of the Church called to settle important disputes of doctrine and discipline. These are councils of the Roman Catholic Church, but the first seven ecumenical councils of the Church are accepted as authoritative by the Eastern Orthodox Churches.

Ecumenism—From the Greek *oikoumene*, "the whole inhabited world." Any attempts to deal with the relations between different Christian groups, or to think of ways in which divisions might be overcome.

Eucharist—The sacrament whereby the

bread and wine really or symbolically becomes the body and blood of Christ.

Excommunication—The formal cutting off of a person from the life of the Church and the reception of the sacraments.

Fathers of the Church—Early church authors (e.g. Ambrose, Jerome, Augustine, Basil, Gregory of Nyssa) who explained the Scriptures with great acuity and whose writings thus gained authority within the church community.

Final Judgment—In contrast to the particular judgment given at death, this is the time, at Christ's Second Coming, when the fate of human beings will be decided for all eternity.

Hymn—A religious poem set to music and sung as part of worship.

Iconostasis—A screen, ornamented with rows of icons, which separates the nave from the altar in many Eastern Churches. It is beyond this screen that the bread and wine are transformed into the body and blood of Christ during the Divine Liturgy.

Incarnation—The mystery believed by Christians that God became man by the union of the divine and human natures in the person of Jesus Christ.

Indulgence—The removal in full or in part of the punishment due to sins. Even after sins have been forgiven through the sacrament of penance and true contrition, sinners still owe some form of recompense for the sins they have committed.

Infallibility—The belief held by Roman Catholics that the pope cannot make an error in matters of faith and morals when he speaks by virtue of his office.

Messiah—An anointed king promised to the Jewish people as someone who would lead them to overcome their enemies. *Messiah*, in Hebrew, means "anointed one." The corresponding word in Greek is *Christos*, or, in English, "Christ."

Monk—A religious man following the Rule of Saint Benedict who spends most of his day in prayer and who attempts to lead a perfect Christian life by taking vows pledging himself to poverty, chastity, and obedience.

Novena—Roman Catholic devotions consisting of prayers or services held on nine consecutive days or weeks honoring Mary, the Mother of Jesus, or the saints.

Pentecost—The feast celebrated by Christian believers, commemorating Christ's sending of the Holy Spirit to the apostles. It is considered by Christians to be the birthday of the Church.

Pharisee—The Hebrew for "separatist." One of a group of observant Jews, beginning before the time of Jesus and continuing with important leadership roles afterwards. The Pharisees helped develop an elaborate system of oral laws to apply the written law of Moses to Jewish life after the Roman conquest of their homeland and the destruction of the Temple.

Protestant—A term first used in 1529 to express the protest of several princes and representatives of fourteen German cities against an attempt by the Roman Catholic emperor Charles V to limit the practice of Lutheranism within the Holy Roman Empire. The term later was extended to Lutherans and other Christians who separated from Roman Catholicism.

Resurrection—The belief that Christ rose from the dead after his crucifixion and death. It is the guarantee, according to Saint Paul, that the followers of Christ will similarly survive physical death and be joined with their heavenly Father.

Roman Curia—The group that serves as the pope's administrative arm. It consists of the secretariat of state, which assists the pope most directly in governing the Church, and a number of other departments, each of which has a specific function.

Sacraments—Signs of divine help or grace, needed for living a good Christian life, through which God confers the help of grace he promises.

Sadducee—A member of the priestly family, who believed in the religious authority of the Torah, or first five books of the Bible alone, and who opposed the new interpretations advanced by the Pharisees.

Schism—A split between two churches that does not involve the denial of any truth of the faith. Such a denial of a truth of the Christian faith would be called heresy.

Scribes—The learned class among the Jews and the official authorities on the written law and the oral traditions. The function of the priests was to care for ceremonies; the function of the scribes was to clarify doctrine or teaching. Generally, the scribes sided with the Pharisees rather than the Sadducees.

Second Vatican Council—A worldwide church council for Roman Catholics opened by Pope John XXIII in 1962 for bringing Roman Catholic life and teaching up to date. Vatican II was closed by Pope Paul VI in 1965.

Seminary—A school for training members of the clergy for the Roman Catholic and Eastern Orthodox Churches.

Trinity—The Christian belief that in God there are three persons: the Father, the Son (who became man in Christ), and the Holy Spirit.

Vernacular—Local language permitted to be used in religious ceremonies instead of the offical Latin and Greek languages that had been used by Roman Catholics and Eastern Orthodox Churches for centuries.

FOR FURTHER READING

Beinert, Wolfgang (ed.). *Handbook of Catholic Theology*. New York: The Crossroad Publishing Company, 1995.

Breck, John. *The Sacred Gift of Life*. Crestwood, N.Y.: St. Vladimir's Seminary Press, 1998.

Fahey, Michael. *Orthodox and Catholic, Sister Churches*. Milwaukee, Wisc.: Marquette University Press, 1996.

Florensky, Pavel. *Iconostasis*. Crestwood, N.Y.: St. Vladimir's Seminary Press, 1996.

Glazier, Michael (ed.). *The Encyclopedia of American Catholic History*. Collegeville, Minn.: The Liturgical Press, 1997.

Maloney, George A. *Gold, Frankincense, and Myrrh: An Introduction to Eastern Christian Spirituality*. New York: The Crossroad Publishing Company, 1997.

Sobrino, Jon. *The Principle of Mercy: Taking the Crucified People from the Cross*. Maryknoll, N.Y.: Orbis Books, 1994.

Stravinskas, Peter. *Our Sunday Visitor's Catholic Encyclopedia*. Huntington, Ind.: Our Sunday Visitor, Inc., 1998.

Vasileios of Stavronikita, Archimandrite. *Hymn of Entry: Liturgy and Life in the Orthodox Church*. Crestwood, N.Y.: St. Vladimir's Seminary Press, 1984.

INDEX